WAYS TO MANAGE BETTER

Andrew Leigh is a senior partner in Maynard Leigh Associates, the development and consultancy service. MLA's clients include Sainsbury's, Ericssons, the London Stock Exchange, EMAP, and Coopers and Lybrand. The author worked as a business journalist on the *Observer*, was for many years a senior manager in the public sector and now advises companies on management development. He is an expert on team development and leadership. He has written many other books and is a Fellow of the Institute of Personnel and Development.

20
WAYS TO
MANAGE
BETTER

Andrew Leigh

Second Edition

INSTITUTE OF PERSONNEL AND DEVELOPMENT

For my parents, George and Rene Leigh

First published 1984
Reprinted 1985, 1987, 1991, 1992
Second edition 1995

Typeset by The Comp-Room, Aylesbury
Printed in Great Britain by
The Short Run Press, Exeter

British Library Cataloguing in Publication Data

*A catalogue record for this book is available from the
British Library*

ISBN 0-85292-591-3 2nd edition
(ISBN 0-85292-334-1 1st edition)

The views expressed in this book are the author's own, and may not
necessarily reflect those of the IPD.

**INSTITUTE OF PERSONNEL
AND DEVELOPMENT**

IPD House, Camp Road, London SW19 4UX
Tel: 0181 971 9000   Fax: 0181 263 3333
Registered office as above. Registered Charity No. 1038333
A company limited by guarantee. Registered in England No. 2931892

Contents

This revised edition is dedicated to Michael, my business partner for several years. During that time we have continually learned from each other and built a successful company. He certainly changed my life and my main consolation is that I have probably done the same for him.

Introduction

Ten years is a long time for a management book to survive. That *20 Ways* continues to serve a need reflects the fact that busy managers still value distilled wisdom. So while this is no academic tome it does give you the essence of various core areas of management.

When the book first appeared (in 1984) I found myself defending its intentions. Surely most experts and professionals would reject the attempt to refine often complex subjects into a dozen or so pages? The continued appeal of *20 Ways* and its translation into several other languages have dealt with such reservations.

The original audience for the book was junior or middle managers. However, *20 Ways* has discreetly crept onto the shelves of many top managers too, which probably says more about them than the book.

The first edition was written while I was a busy line manager and wondering how to do the job better. My responsibilities increased until I was (nominally, at least), in charge of scores of different teams, and I therefore have absolute sympathy with any manager who feels there are never enough hours in the day to read about management as well as do it. Now that I run my own development and consultancy service I am even more aware of the pressures preventing one reading anything remotely called a management book. Yet to improve as a manager one still needs help and stimulus from somewhere. That remains the purpose of *20 Ways*.

Despite many impressive multimedia sources on some of the basic management skills, to say nothing of countless training courses, not everyone wants to learn that way. Sitting in a train, a plane or just at home in front of a fire can be an equally important way of gaining fresh insight into doing one's job.

Structure

In revising *20 Ways* I have rewritten most of it, brought the material up to date and altered many of the topics covered in the original edition. The present ones are as mainstream as you can get, although there will always be arguments for including or excluding some topic. Please regard this as a resource, rather than a textbook – which means you are not expected to read it from cover to cover, though do so if you want.

The book is now in three distinct parts: Business Skills, Team Skills and Personal Skills. This division has a certain logic, although there are inevitable overlaps. However, the sections emphasise the realities of working life and the reasons why you may need to make your own decisions about what particular skills you require. Thus an almost unstated theme is taking responsibility for your own development – not just career development, whatever that may mean nowadays, but also your growth as an effective person in a working environment. The latter is now the defining factor rather than 'the job', which is rapidly losing its traditional meaning.

No matter how generous and far sighted, few employers will provide sufficient off-site training or formal learning experiences to promote your growth as a manager and as a human being. Increasingly employers are looking to individuals themselves to take some responsibility for their own growth; hence the continued relevance of the kind of material offered in this book.

Tomorrow's world

As a manager you are facing one of the most challenging periods you might have chosen in the last 100 years to do this kind of work. Whole new industries are emerging at a frenetic rate. Genetics, materials, digital technology, information and many others are going to transform the world in which you and organisations live. Thus any written advice on management is theoretically already dated. Yet some things never change. Core competencies seem destined to go on being refined and given a new focus. That focus is likely to be away from merely managing, ie coping, towards activities that can justly be termed leadership.

It will not be enough to be a 'manager'. Having completed their restructuring, downsizing and re-engineering cycles, organisations will need to address the future more seriously than they generally do right now. To succeed as a manager you will be confronting fundamental issues such as: how can you help transform your organisation; how might the company take the lead and determine industry standards; how might you assist the enterprise identify markets that currently do not exist; which people can help the organisation do better than merely survive and instead thrive?

Competition, often on a global scale, will be an even more important driving force for both organisations and those who run them. The pace of competition is accelerating, and more and more companies are facing it from unexpected quarters. Organisations and managers need to respond in more sophisticated and creative ways.

Competition – the Driving Forces and Critical Success Factors*

The driving forces

- customers demanding products and services increasingly customised to their needs
- customer satisfaction standards which are increasingly established by global competition
- reductions in international trade barriers
- industrialisation of Pacific-rim countries
- slow growth in the mature economies
- new overseas competitors in mature production and service sectors
- technology which is rapidly changing and easily transferable
- public-sector financial constraints, political pressures for higher value for money and privatisation or market testing
- communities becoming more concerned about the effects of economic development on the environment and social well-being

How organisations are responding

- highly differentiated goods and services
- customer-led organisations
- 'step' change and continuous improvement of products, processes, and services
- quicker response times
- lower costs and sustainable profits
- flexibility from people and technology
- investing in and developing the core competences of people

How this is affecting the way people are organised and managed

- decentralisation and development of decision making
- slimmer and flatter management structures

cont.

- total quality and lean organisational initiatives
- fewer specialists directly employed
- developing a flexible workforce
- more project-based and cross-functional initiatives and teamworking
- empowered rather than command structures
- partnership approach to supplier links

What this means for employees

- customer-orientation to meet the needs of both internal and external customers
- greater self-management and responsibility for individuals and teams
- contributing to the continuous improvement of processes, products and services
- commitment to personal training, development and adaptability

What does this mean for managers?

- facilitating, co-ordinating roles
- greater interpersonal, team leadership and motivational skills
- openness, fairness, and a partnership in employment relations
- managing constructively the interests of groups of employees and their collective and individual representation
- ensuring part-time and temporary employees and those contracted to supply services are fully integrated.

* Adapted from *Managing People – the Changing Frontiers*, published by the IPD.

Because *20 Ways* is not primarily aimed at senior managers, it devotes only a limited space to strategic thinking. The latter deals with the organisation's future and what it wants to be, yet by being deliberately concerned with this, you immediately start to distinguish yourself from many other managers around you. 'Strategic intent' is a way of describing more precisely what the organisation plans to achieve. To be a successful manager you need gradually to develop your capacity to identify and understand the organisation's strategic intent. Only then can you contribute to the broader picture that is the responsibility of successful senior managers.

Strategic thinking does not mean you must become a corporate planner or outguess the chairman. It does mean continually asking yourself (and others) questions about the future of the organisation, its markets, its industry, and what will keep it alive and vital. Doing so will undoubtedly help you to be a better manager.

Better than what, though? Better than many of your colleagues who have their heads down in solely day-to-day issues, who are trapped in short-term thinking and a narrow perspective.

20 Ways is not merely a survival guide: it is aimed at your personal growth.

Part One

Business Skills

1 *one*

Setting Objectives

When the Hubble space telescope failed it was a major scientific disaster. Millions of dollars had been spent building it, then hoisting it aloft. It was supposed to provide revelations about the far universe. But Hubble did not work.

As one sceptical senator commented, the Hubble trouble meant this costly investment was 'a turkey'. Yet a few months later this same senator was proudly showing pictures from a newly revived Hubble that were stunning in their focus and clarity.

To get Hubble working again the National Aeronautics and Space Administration (NASA) set tough and highly specific objectives. Up to 10 major component changes were needed in space. Astronauts faced problems from jammed doors to replacement parts as big as a telephone box.

NASA met its objectives in full. Reviving Hubble was a triumph and possibly saved the entire future of the space agency. It was a highly visible demonstration of the power of objective setting with systematic follow through.

Setting objectives is part of every managers' job. Once this was treated formally it was dubbed Management By Objectives (MBO). MBO sank beneath its own weight of bureaucracy and excessive rigidity.

Today, objective setting is seen as an art, not a science. It is a way of steering the organisation into the future and guiding what people do in an orderly manner. Not setting objectives is wasteful and leads to confusion. Yet equally how one sets them is a critical factor in making them useful.

If you really want to survive as a manager well into the twenty-first century, consider objectives in their broadest sense. They are not merely about measurable goals for which people choose to become accountable. They are also concerned with helping you and the organisation handle the future.

No matter how brilliantly you set objectives, they can still be fundamentally the wrong ones. Successful objective setting incorporates the organisation's future, it relates to what the enterprise wants to be. Objectives that merely relate to your personal agenda are unlikely to be effective.

What is an objective?

An objective is another way of saying aim, or final result. Objectives are also often called goals or aims, although sometimes the last two are rather broader. Goals are where you want to get to, objectives are usually the more detailed ways of achieving them.

Trying to distinguish between goals and objectives frequently leads to confusion and different organisations have their own approaches. Since goals, objectives and aims are so often used interchangeably we will not make a major distinction between them here.

Objectives answer the simple question:

● What are you trying to achieve?

Objective setting is a *process* rather than a *system*. Organisations adopting formal objective setting usually set certain rules for creating, documenting and then monitoring them.

Objectives are large statements of intent. For example, to:

● double our turnover in two years
● reduce complaints to three per five hundred customers
● increase our profit margin by 20 per cent within 18 months
● obtain a 30 per cent market share by next June
● shut this production line with minimum disruption to other lines
● improve the retention of staff by 15 per cent within one year
● open a branch office in New York within five years.

Objectives are usually then broken into smaller chunks. These chunks are targets and are the nuts and bolts of the whole process. While practically anyone can set a broad aim, part of the skill is converting it into a whole series of practical steps that mesh together to achieve the overall result.

So, for example, an objective such as 'improve our profit margin' may need converting into several smaller targets:

Target 1   Increase our sale price to the customer by 10 per cent.
Target 2   Identify all overheads and their proportion of the total.
Target 3   Reduce selected overheads by 30 per cent within one year.

Target 4   Launch at least one new product that attracts an exceptional margin.

Organisational targets need converting into still smaller ones that ultimately reduce to ones that each person can understand in terms of their own job. They are basically milestones for judging progress.

Vision, Objectives (goals or aims) and Targets

Vision: the grand picture – what the organisation aspires to

Example: To be the bank everyone considers going to first

Objectives: the steps to achieving the vision

Example:

Objective 1   Have more high street branches than any competitor by the end of the decade.

Objective 2   Offer the fastest counter service in Britain, as measured by industry norms, by the end of the decade.

Objective 3   Give all customers the service they need, plus a bit more – as measured by independent consumer studies – by the end of next year.

Targets: the more detailed results required for reaching an objective

Example:

Objective 1   Have more high street branches than any competitor by the end of the decade.

Target 1   Identify 700 suitable properties for purchase or lease by year end.

Target 2   Complete purchase on 200 properties by year end.

Target 3   Refurbish at least 20 per cent of all new premises by year end.

Target 4   Open to the public 30+ new branches by year end.

Writing down objectives is an essential part of the process. Keeping them all in one's head is seldom either desirable or necessary. It is also wasteful since the act of writing them down helps clarify what will happen, by when, by whom and so on.

Develop your objective setting skills and you will almost certainly increase your personal effectiveness. Others will see you as someone who is organised and efficient. It really pays to model good behaviour and show the way with objective setting.

A formal objective setting system

- helps achieve specific results that are defined in advance
- provides a way of co-ordinating action
- focuses on the kernel of a manager's job – to get results
- improves communication between a manager and others
- acts as a tool for clarifying results
- explains what is expected from people
- provides a control and monitoring mechanism.

It is pointless having objectives without knowing whether or not they are being achieved. An essential element of any formal objective setting process is regular feedback on:

- How quickly one is progressing towards the aim
- How close the end result is
- What still needs doing.

Who sets them?

It used to be assumed that managers set objectives, leaving it to others to make them happen. While this still happens in some organisations the process is increasingly becoming a more participative one.

The dilemma of whether to make objective setting a top down or bottom up process is one you need to resolve in your own mind sooner rather than later. While this decision will often be made for you by the organisation's own rules, you will retain considerable scope for involving people in devising their own personal objectives.

To obtain the most from objective setting it is usually best done in conjunction with those who must try to achieve the results. Rather than imposing objectives, good managers involve people in choosing what is possible and desirable. Even when certain objectives are presented as non-negotiable aims, the process of breaking them into more detailed targets is still best done collaboratively.

In formal objective setting systems, senior management is expected to decide such basics as the company vision, its core mission, values and so on. However, people have been increasingly questioning the effectiveness of this top down process. After all, an organisation consists of people, who are its main source of competitive advantage. Cascading objectives down through the whole organisation has met growing problems as organisations have changed in terms of structure and ways of working.

A bottom up approach is attractive because it allows more people to have a say in what the organisation should be doing. However, it is extremely time consuming and few companies can make this approach work without a radical overhaul of culture as well as structure.

To make objective setting work from the bottom up you need to be highly organised, giving guidance to people on the need to focus on results. They also need help distinguishing between minor changes that demand little effort and few resources, and those with more substantial implications.

To make objective setting work from the bottom upwards ask questions such as:

● What activities would have the greatest impact on your/our efficiency?

● How will we measure success or know whether it is being achieved?

● How do you need to be developed personally in order to make a bigger contribution?

● Why have previous objectives not been reached and what lessons flow from that experience?

Smart objectives

How do you set really useful objectives? An excellent system is called the SMART method. SMART objectives are:

Stretching; Measurable; Acceptable; Recorded; Time-limited

Stretching

Stretching objectives use people's full potential. They lead people to reach for what may seem beyond their immediately apparent abilities. Such aims are not necessarily attainable, or in some cases realistic. With a stretching objective you may not know whether it will definitely be achieved. Such an objective is therefore *risky*.

Only in trying to reach the objective will it eventually be apparent whether it was realistic. So a stretching objective

- poses a challenge
- excites people
- taps people's creative, inner resources.

Measurable

A *measurable* objective is highly specific, the opposite of woolly. It is probably measurable if you can answer the simple question:

- Will I know whether or not this goal has been achieved?

Measurability means deciding *by how much* the desired objective has been reached. For instance the objective 'to raise profits' is vague. The essentials are unclear: by how much and by when? What is missing is a reliable *measure* of profitability.

You can make to an important contribution to objective setting by constantly seeking measurability. Some senior managers have argued that 'if you cannot measure it, you cannot manage it'. While this is an extreme position, it certainly helps to focus on the importance of making objectives sufficiently specific, to know whether or not they are being achieved and at what rate.

Acceptable

An *acceptable* objective is one to which people are prepared to commit themselves fully. It is pointless setting one if no one else will really try to achieve it. You therefore need to discover ways to enrol people in the desirability of achieving a particular aim. You do this by tapping into their natural energy and enthusiasm.

To really strive to achieve an objective people have to make it their own; they have to 'own' it. Otherwise they may only go through the motions of trying to achieve it. So what will it take for people to accept an objective? Somehow they must come to believe it is both *desirable and achievable*.

First it must be *personally desirable* for them in some way, not just desirable for the organisation. Secondly, people need to believe it can be achieved with suitable effort, ingenuity, time and resources. It may never be truly achievable, but at the time of acceptance people are willing to strive for it. For example a sales manager may set his team the objective of increasing sales by 50 per cent next year. If the team believes it is unachievable and cannot be inspired to try and reach it, they will reject it, even if it is formally imposed. So at some level, an achievable goal is seen by those striving for it as realistic.

Most people love a challenge and devising demanding objectives is part of being an effective manager. It may not always matter whether the objective is ultimately unattainable, so long as you can somehow convince people it might be, and is therefore worth striving for.

Recorded

Objectives need to be *Recorded* to avoid losing track of what you are trying to achieve. You can keep a single objective in your head; it is harder with five or six. Develop a reliable way of keeping track of each by recording

● what you are aiming to achieve
● whether you are achieving it
● the extent to which you are succeeding (or failing) to reach it.

Record objectives and their related targets in a special file or notebook, or as part of a formal documentation system. You may also find it helpful to post a team's objectives on display.

Recording objectives and monitoring their progress encourages clarity about what is happening. However, excessive detail can sow confusion. List the more detailed information about the complex stages of a major project on separate schedules.

Time-limited

Objectives should be *time-limited* so people know when they must achieve them. Time boundaries makes good use of resources by focusing people's attention on a definite end date. Time limits:

● clarify urgency
● focus team energy
● communicate goals to non-team members
● set standards of performance.

Objectives without time boundaries usually degenerate into mere wishing. Without a sense of urgency the natural human tendency is to tackle other, more pressing, matters.

Select time boundaries to which everyone can relate. Broad corporate objectives may relate to a decade but these must be converted to more specific time periods. For example, in SmithKline Beecham, the health care giant, there is a grand 25-year vision, yet the senior management has introduced what they call the 10,3,1 principle. There is is a 10-year set of objectives, supported by more detailed three-year ones, and even more specific one-year ones.

The whole point of time limits is that people and organisations are expected to achieve particular results within them. Deadlines that are constantly ignored or not taken seriously will undermine the whole objective setting process. To get the best from people, encourage the ground rule of never missing deadlines, except in truly exceptional circumstances.

Adapt time boundaries to reflect changing circumstances. This means using evidence about what is happening in the real world, rather than sticking blindly to established deadlines. Inevitably, some will need altering in response to new situations.

Further reading

ORDIORNE G. S. *The Human Side of Management.* Hemel Hempstead, Lexington Books, 1987

2 *two*

Recruitment and Selection

Placing her crystal ball on the boardroom table, the fortune teller stared into the murky depths. 'You would be unwise to employ Mr Johnson as your Sales Director; he has a dark secret not declared on his CV.'

She was followed by a smartly dressed man who entered holding a clip board. Using the handwriting on Mr Johnson's letter and application form he revealed that 'he's an outgoing sort of chap, likes to eat and drink, probably a bit of a womaniser. He is a latent homosexual and is a bit too insensitive for this job.'

So far, no company admits to employing a fortune teller for staff selections and virtually none, in Britain at least, uses graphology. Yet given the poor track record of many company appointments, they might just as well have resorted to such dubious measures.

A poor recruitment choice could cost your company dearly. For example, if someone leaves within the first six months it can cost the company up to three times their annual salary in finders fees, recruitment advertising and the whole appointment process. Worse though, it may affect your own career prospects. If your role is to obtain results from people, selecting the right ones is essential. Even if there are personnel experts to support you, recruitment and selection is a prime management responsibility.

Give recruitment and selection a fair share of your attention and it will certainly repay you. You will reduce the amount of time and energy spent on trying to deal with 'square pegs' stuck in round holes.

Try to view recruitment and selection in the wider context of the organisation's future. What does the organisation want to be? What are its aspirations? What is its strategic intent? Hence what capabilities will the enterprise need in the future?

Taking a short term and narrow view of recruitment and selection may fill a vacancy, it will not help the organisation thrive. Thus an important strategic issue to consider is how your recruitment and selection activity can contribute to longer term business goals. This more far reaching vision will set you apart from managers who take a more myopic view of their job.

Increasingly 'the job' is being replaced by a more fluid concept of work to be done. Job descriptions, once the heart of employing people, are giving way to less inflexible means of describing broad tasks and skills, attitudes and responses to changing situations.

Faced with filling an existing vacancy, your main focus will probably be on getting someone who can do the work. Yet recruitment is also part of a wider process arising from the organisation's longer term needs:

The Process

Stage 1 Creation of a business plan and company aims

Stage 2 Resource analysis – identifying numbers and types of people, skills and other human resource requirements, using the results from succession planning; often termed manpower planning

Stage 3 Work analysis: specifying the new work and deciding content; preparation of descriptions of the tasks to be done (usually called job descriptions)

Stage 4 Candidate specification: describing the sort of person who would fit the job

Stage 5 Attracting candidates: advertising, job forums etc.

Stage 6 Listing: initial matching of candidates to the requirements, short listing

Stage 7 Selection: meeting the candidates; interviewing, testing

Stage 8 Deciding and making the appointment

Stage 9 Induction.

The business plan

If you are unsure where the organisation is headed it is hard to make any sense of recruitment needs. You can only respond to specific vacancies and take a short term view. Effective managers have a longer term horizon. They ask questions such as 'Do we need to recruit at all?' The business plan is the starting point for clarifying the organisation's requirement for staff.

Resource analysis (manpower planning)

Even without professional help with resource analysis, you can certainly consider two basic types of issue: recruitment avoidance and recruitment need. The former is when you systematically check whether there is any way to avoid further recruitment. You ask questions such as:

- Why do I need to recruit – is an appointment really necessary?
- Could the work be reallocated to existing staff?
- Can the work be divided up or eliminated?
- Are existing staff using their full potential?

You may also need to explore why the previous employee left and whether simply recruiting a replacement will solve the problem. Ask questions such as:

- What is the resource requirement now and over the next few years?
- What is the nature of the work that needs doing?
- What kind of person would do the work (fill the job)?
- Where could we find the right kind of recruit(s)?
- What will we need to pay to attract the right candidate(s)?
- What special training will be necessary?

Work analysis

Work analysis can help you select more productive employees by identifying the main themes in the tasks to be done. It also lists what attributes people need. This is therefore where you systematically explore the nature of the work itself.

For existing jobs you obtain such information for instance by asking those doing them to write down in detail their duties and categorising them in some way. Alternatively someone else may study the person doing the work and produce a detailed report on what is involved.

You may need information on:

- *work requirement* such as basic education and pre-job training needs, on the job training required, skills required, physical effort needed, mental demands etc.
- *responsibility* for materials, equipment, decisions, supervision of others, safety, contact with the public etc.
- *working conditions* such as humidity, temperature, noise, hazards, location etc.

There are many ways to obtain information for work analysis including film, written records, observation, structured and open-ended questionnaires, diaries, interviews and job shadowing.

Work analysis is a field in its own right, and includes techniques such as studying critical incidents, repertory grid and occupational analysis. You will probably never conduct these studies personnally, but will rely on outside specialists to provide the information.

The next step is to create a work or job description. Usually this will consist of one or more pages summarising the purpose, scope, grade, duties and responsibilities and relationships that form the job. It would not normally include anything about the skills or personality required.

Job descriptions are still used but are increasingly seen as inflexible in a fast changing work environment. It is better to describe broad activities and areas of responsibility. A short and clear work description lies at the heart of good recruitment since it helps to match the person to the work and the work to the person.

Candidate specification

When you have described the work to be done, next identify what kind of person you need. Candidate specifications list the essential attributes that are required, such as a university degree, a high level of manual dexterity or an ability to use a spread sheet. Distinguish between:

- essential candidate requirements
- desirable candidate requirements.

Avoid specifying requirements in vague 'management speak'. For example, saying you want someone keen and well motivated has little value. No one is likely to want someone who is idle, apathetic and unmotivated.

Attracting candidates

It is usually easier to attract candidates than to select the right one. Before looking outside, check whether there is someone already on the payroll who could do the work. Even with extra training this will still usually be cheaper than recruiting an outsider.

If you know the sort of person you want – for example a new graduate – it pays to discover what will attract and retain them. Pay, for example, may be less critical in determining whether people apply than whether the job is interesting and has good prospects. One large food company lost half its new graduates within six months of hiring them because it was recruiting extroverts and sending them unsupported to remote places.

Think carefully about your desired candidate and advertise in a medium they are likely to see. For instance, you may obtain rather different candidates by advertising in the *Guardian* from the ones you would get from *The Times*.

Successful job advertisements clarify the nature of the job and the person you are seeking. Take a personal interest in the job advertisement and do not leave it entirely to personnel specialists.

Recruitment adverts

Give priority to:

- the work being interesting
- advancement and prospects
- earnings and security
- personal involvement
- relationships and working with colleagues
- education and training prospects.

Give less priority to:

- holiday entitlement
- travel opportunities
- sports and social facilities
- status symbols
- fringe benefits
- prestige of the organisation.

Offering the name of a person to write to also encourages replies. Avoid using box numbers, as this tends to deter people from applying. To avoid a mountain of applications give enough information for people to exclude themselves.

Make sure the copy is legal and without racial, sexual and other forms of discrimination. Be wary also of unnecessary ageism creeping in: this may cut you off from some highly effective candidates.

Listing

With more than half a dozen applicants you can develop a:

- preliminary short list

- reserve list
- reject list.

Treat with respect everyone who applies. They all deserve a courteous reply if they have taken the trouble to contact you. Even if the reply is a general rejection, make it friendly. For example, wish the person good luck in their search for a job.

Selection

The three methods of selection favoured by most organisations are the job application form, references and the interview. However there are plenty of other methods to consider, including:

- psychological tests
- ability tests
- assessment centres
- group exercises
- work sample tests.

Accuracy of recruitment methods ranked from highest to lowest:

- assessment centres for promotion
- structured interviews
- work samples
- ability tests
- assessment centres for performance
- biodata
- personality tests
- unstructured interviews
- references.

Two thirds of British employers always take up references and only a handful never do. Better still may be a chat with the person's present employer. You will often learn far more than from any written reference. However, not all organisations permit this practice.

The interview

Three things most managers think they do well in life are: drive, make love and interview. Interviews, however, have a generally poor record for effective selection. In fact, it is the unstructured interview used without much other support that works so badly.

The interview remains the most popular recruitment tool and virtually all organisations use it. To maximise your chances of success in using interviews:

● avoid relying solely on the interview as your main means of selection
● structure interviews into a logical sequence covering key areas.

Structured interviews bring more discipline to the encounter. You can further enhance its effectiveness by using key behaviour questions and situation questions.

Key behaviour enquiries   These identify critical elements of successful job performance. They are converted into probing interview questions for exploring both likely job behaviour and job performance. Identifying critical elements can be complicated and is best done by experts.

Situation questions   These also use critical elements but are more future orientated. You identify what behaviour patterns matter and then ask, 'What would you do in this situation?' As with key behaviour enquiries, you rate the candidate on a prearranged scale.

Key question   A key question to always ask a candidate right at the start is:

● If you were offered this job would you take it?

A few candidates may virtually eliminate themselves by their hesitancy.

Tests

Psychological tests and group exercises can increase your knowledge of a candidate and improve the selection process. However, you will usually benefit from professional help in using such methods. Many tests for example require a licensed administrator.

Tests are also expensive, but so is choosing the wrong candidate. Restrict your short list to a manageable number so that you minimise the costs of testing. They may prolong the selection process by several weeks.

Work sample tests   Work sample tests are a good way of checking whether the person can do what they say they can do. For example, if someone says they can type using Word Perfect, let them demonstrate. You will soon know whether this is true.

Try giving the candidates examples of real work problems and ask them how they would tackle them. 'What would you do if . . . ?'

What to Avoid during Interviews

Primary effect. You jump to conclusions about a candidate – research does not support the idea that interviewers accept or reject candidates in the first few minutes

Expectancy effect. Your initial expectations about someone stems from the application form and prejudices your final decision

Confirmation bias effect. You ask questions which actively seek information to confirm your initial impression; this may prevent you asking more probing and important ones

Fixed views effect. You have a preconceived notion of your ideal candidate and end up seeking to match candidates to this notion; it may prevent you selecting someone who is excellent yet different

Halo or horns effect. You consistently interpret information and rate candidates too positively or too negatively

Contrast effect. Your decisions are affected by candidates you saw earlier and by pre-set employment quotas

Negative bias. You are more influenced by negative information from candidates than positive information

Clone syndrome. You keep looking for candidates who are like you in terms of background, education, personality and attitudes

The liking bias. You select candidates because you personally like them and are consequently less objective in your ratings of ability.

Decision and appointment

If you are faced with several candidates who seem fairly evenly matched you may be uncertain about whom to appoint. Rather than toss a coin or make an instinctive decision, try a second or even third interview. This may seem excessive but the cost of a wrong decision is high.

If you still cannot choose between two equal candidates, give them a job related task to perform and have some clear criteria established *in advance* for how you will assess the results.

Before making the final decision, take up any references and conduct any security checks required in your organisation. Before confirming the appointment, be sure the person has accepted the normal terms of employment and the pay on offer.

Induction

The final stage is helping the person settle into their new job. Careful attention to induction:

● establishes a favourable attitude towards the employer

● helps the person reach their maximum effectiveness in the shortest time.

Induction is a sound investment that soon pays for itself.

Further reading

COOK M. *Personnel Selection and Productivity.* (2nd edition.) Chichester, John Wiley and Sons, 1993

3 *three*

Appraisal

'How am I doing?' Every employee is entitled to know the answer to this question. Ways of answering it, however, have been changing. Although appraisal is widely interpreted, it usually means:

● written assessments of employees carried out systematically and at regular intervals

In most organisations, it is the manager who 'owns' this process and makes all the necessary judgements about the employee. Where appraisals merely involve one person commenting on another, they seldom work well. In a survey of West Midland companies, for instance, more than two out of three companies, several of which were household names, reported having difficulty with performance appraisal.

A formal annual appraisal interview between a manager and subordinate is now increasingly being supplemented or even replaced by more effective approaches. With the increasing requirement for managers to take on responsibility for developing their staff, delegating this task to personnel or human resource specialists is difficult. Such staff are either no longer employed or now offer mainly internal consultancy services. So line managers and others with responsibility for getting the best from people are having to face a changing approach to making appraisals work. One reason why many resist conducting traditional appraisals is the potential harm to the relationship between them and their staff.

With flatter organisations, fewer layers and less direct supervision, different and rather healthier attitudes towards appraisal are emerging. Rules, and obedience to them, are playing a less important part in many successful enterprises. With a more organic, less mechanistic, view of organisations, appraisal offers two distinct benefits:

- It helps individuals maximise their potential.
- It links individual performance to the achievement of corporate goals.

Issues affecting appraisal

Two important issues that will affect your whole approach to appraisals are *organisation culture* and the much wider challenge of *performance management*.

Culture

What holds an organisation together through constant change is a strong set of common beliefs about what it is about and what it wants to become. It is in this context that you should conduct appraisals..

Performance management

While appraisals need to focus on the individual's immediate work performance, they are also about whether the person is demonstrating through their actions support for the company culture, values and aspirations. You are asking not so much 'Are you doing what I asked?' as 'What are you doing to support our vision and our values?'

This wider view of appraisal is what *performance management* is all about. It focuses more on obtaining results from people than on merely judging them. You do this by

- giving direction
- recognising and rewarding
- discovering employee concerns
- offering and receiving feedback
- increasing job satisfaction.

Thus the demands on you are greater than in traditional appraisal interviews that tend to be one way and highly judgemental. In the new style performance management you may play many roles, including leader, facilitator, negotiator, counsellor and even researcher.

The dialogue you hold with someone who reports to you is also different from old style appraising. Old style appraisals tend to be problem centred, with you the manager offering suggestions for how the individual can improve. Performance management is more future orientated, with you offering a dialogue which the other person finds open, and in which you are enquiring, receiving and encouraging.

Appraisal is therefore not something 'done' to someone. Instead, the relationship is based on mutual respect and is more a form of partnership, based on discussion and eliminating inhibitions to communication.

Damned by Deming

The arch high priest of 'quality', W.E. Deming condemned performance appraisal as one of the seven deadly sins of management practice. He saw it as damaging because it blamed variations in company performance on individuals rather than the system of management control. He argued that by focusing on the individual's performance, management merely creates morale problems.

Yet individual responsibility within a team setting is also at the core of the new approach to running organisations. Increasingly managers realise that many important aspects of the organisation are not entirely measurable and that effort and behaviour are just as important as more hard edged, quantified results.

A rejection of the individualistic approach stems from the belief that you simply cannot disentangle a person's contribution from the wider systems: teams, technology, structures and so on. For example, it is no good blaming an administrator for not processing enough invoices if the computer system is badly designed and slow.

Decentralisation, autonomy and self-management are increasingly the norm. Formal appraisal systems based solely on a manager's judgements are therefore prone to disempower people. A better way of getting the best from people is by helping them be more effective, which is the starting point of performance management. First you set performance requirements, monitor whether they have been achieved and only then conduct an appraisal.

If your organisation has a formal appraisal system you will probably be restricted in how you proceed. At least ensure that you are clear about its aims so that you can explain them to the person on the receiving end.

Increase your chances of a successful appraisal encounter by giving your main attention to helping the person arrive at their own judgements about their performance. This is empowerment. That is, you review performance so as to make the experience helpful, rather than judgemental, critical or punishing.

Keep your appraisals simple. Mountains of personality profiles, psychometric tests and biodata are no substitute for being able to appraise someone effectively. It would be convenient if the process could be an entirely rigorous, scientific event, controlled by strict rules that everyone understands. However, the reality is otherwise. It is a social experience, an interaction between human beings with many unknowns, and much of it is unpredictable.

Why Conduct Appraisals?

- to make decisions about rewards
- to achieve an improvement in performance
- to show people where they fit and to motivate them
- to identify potential and develop the individual
- for succession planning
- to promote people
- to identify and communicate poor performance.

As an appraiser, adopt a means of monitoring performance and ensure there is an opportunity to meet each person reporting to you.

The most basic tool for this is setting objectives (see Chapter 1). This is an opportunity to agree actions leading to changes or improvements in personal performance.

In the mid-1990s a survey by the Institute of Personnel and Development found a growing interest in appraisal. Organisations introducing appraisal systems did so for some highly specific reasons. The commonest ones were:

- to improve performance
- to identify training needs
- to encourage a manager/worker dialogue.

Less common reasons were to achieve a cultural change, for pay reviews and as part of a quality initiative. The most common benefits from appraisal were:

- improved individual performance
- improved employee communications
- improved employee commitment.

Just under half the organisations said their appraisal arrangements had prompted improved corporate performance. One third felt it had led to increased productivity.

(*Performance Management in the UK*: An Analysis of the Issues, Bevan and Thompson, March 1994)

Several different parties have an interest in making appraisal work. They include you the manager, the person being appraised, team colleagues, senior management and personnel specialists. Because of these varying interests, an individual may view an appraisal as:

- *performance:* What do you think of my work?
- *commitment:* How do you see my involvement?
- *pay:* How will you reward me?
- *potential:* What do you believe I am capable of doing?
- *promotion:* Do I merit advancement?

Cramming all these aspects into a single appraisal interview is likely to prove impossible; there is too much at stake. Consequently, many organisations adopt a dual approach:

- a broad performance management session once a year, tied to the start of the business year, on objective setting, pay and general review
- one or more appraisal meetings to focus on developing the individual.

Some experts and managers argue that linking pay and performance with appraisal is bound to fail, because it focuses mainly on the organisation's needs rather than the individual's.

Performance Management, on the other hand, demands a definite link between pay and performance in appraisals. During the discussion, future directions are agreed and specific objectives set. These are always related to the wider business aims.

How often should you hold an appraisal? Annual meetings alone are too infrequent to make much impact. Effective appraisal involves far more frequent assessments and feedback sessions. This is because it no longer makes sense to see a person's self-development as narrowly restricted to organisational life. Instead you can assume that if you help to develop the individual you will eventually grow the company.

Methods

You can appraise someone by:

- assessing personality
- reviewing job related abilities
- using rating scales
- evaluating individual results
- testing competencies.

Mixing these methods does not necessarily produce an effective approach. One that does seem to work is to combine goal-setting with a discussion about personal development. When to use these methods is always a matter of judgement. It may be helpful to discuss with a personnel or human resource specialist which method would be most appropriate for your particular purpose.

360 degree appraisal

For most managers, appraisal still implies assessing someone who directly reports to them. Yet there is an increasing awareness that peer appraisal is also powerful. Moreover, downward assessment needs to be supplemented by allowing the appraisee to do some appraising of the manager.

Upward Appraisal

Upward appraisal has been gaining favour at American Express. It is separated from pay and other annual assessments.

Managers are shown questionnaires completed by peers and subordinates. The combined scores produce a set of company norms. These allow each manager to compare themselves to their equivalents in the organisation. As one manager explained:

> The first time it's quite daunting. You don't know what you are going to hear. The perceptions of people around you are pretty accurate; they know your weaknesses.

In Federal Express, too, all managers are annually appraised by their subordinates. The results are fed into a system for assessing the managers' own performance. Someone who receives a negative upward appraisal is required to change and faces a reappraisal six months later.

In W.H. Smith staff were asked to rate their managers on 32 attributes including: communicates relevant information to me; plans the work effectively; inspires me to do well; does not impose unrealistic objectives; is courteous.

To make upward and peer appraisal work it almost certainly has to be done anonymously.

With organisations increasingly valuing team work, the role of individual appraisal is being challenged. Appraising someone in isolation from the rest of the team makes only limited sense and the implications are clear. Meaningful appraisals must include a wider perspective.

Rather than relying solely on 'manager analysis' to decide someone's effectiveness, you may need to obtain a broader range of information supplied by team members and others outside it.

Performance management moves appraisal away from a historical look at someone's work with its inevitable emphasis on what went wrong. Instead you give more attention to the future:

- setting key objectives – what the person is accountable for
- agreeing measures and standards to be obtained
- assigning time scales and priorities.

Coaching and counselling

To help employees achieve their performance targets, you should also develop your supportive skills. Instead of being just a directing, controlling, delegating person, you will need to offer practical help and advice to people for achieving results.

The appraisal meeting then becomes more like a coaching or counselling session. By focusing on the longer term, rather than immediate outcomes, the dialogue with the employee may be more equal, more of a two-way conversation.

Further details of this approach can be found in Chapter 4, on coaching.

The appraisal interview

Appraisal is not simply an interview, and certainly not just an annual one. Many elements may contribute to its successful outcome. However, interviews are usually an essential part of the process.

Preparing for an appraisal interview means gathering together both formal and informal information. You may use a questionnaire and informal material such as the views and opinions of those who have been in contact with the person you are meeting.

During the interview put the person at ease by explaining the purpose of the meeting and what will happen. Encourage discussion through open ended rather than closed questions that produce a yes or no response.

Start by asking the person how they see their performance since the last appraisal. If you agree with their assessment say so. Otherwise, remain quiet until they have finished and only then start to share your own

What You Need for the Appraisal Interview

You need an awareness of

- the person's job
- how the job is carried out
- what reasonable versus unreasonable objectives are for someone in the job
- how performance may be limited by the nature of the job itself
- how the job might change
- the purpose of the job within the organisation
- the person's strengths and weaknesses

You also need a list of the questions you want to ask.

OBTAIN

- a copy of the person's job description
- a specification of what kind of person is needed to do that particular job
- performance criteria
- previous objectives
- any available tests such a psychometric data or competency ratings
- any reports from other sources such as customers, internal departments etc.
- a room that is private.

Give the person at least three days' notice before the interview and ensure that they understand its purpose. Explain what is involved and how to prepare. Supply a copy of any appraisal form you will use.

perceptions. Have specific examples or evidence ready to support any adverse comments you make.

Do plenty of listening, summarise regularly, and take detailed notes as you go along. Otherwise you may quickly forget what occured. Once you have agreed aims for the next appraisal period (see Chapter 1 on setting objectives), close the interview, summarising the key points. Agree the next review date and explain what happens next. Thank the person for their participation.

Send any completed appraisal document to the interviewee and retain a copy for yourself. Also, diarise any follow-up action.

Standards

Performance criteria are essential for making sense of appraisals. Unless people know how they are being assessed they are likely to conclude that the whole process is arbitrary and unreliable. It may take weeks or months to create credible standards and they may have to be updated regularly. You may need outside advice on devising these criteria but the best source is the person being appraised.

Standards need to rely on observable facts, rather than mere opinion. You and the employee may need to discuss specific standards jointly, if these have not already been established. Three main types of performance criteria to consider are:

- *measurable or quantifiable results*, such as profit per quarter, sales per month, customers contacted, jobs completed etc.

- *actions that reflect agreed policies and cultural norms*, which may be anything from demonstrating customer care to personal time-keeping, and minimising absences

- *personal qualities and work characteristics*, which may include such intangibles as self-confidence, co-operation, leadership and showing initiative.

Structure

Your meeting also needs a definite structure, so that you both know what territory you are going to cover and in what order.

Appraisal structure

- introduction
- discussing performance strengths
- reviewing areas for personal development
- developing specific plans
- summarising key points and agreed actions

Give thought to

- a convenient time for both parties
- allowing at least 60 to 90 minutes for the interview
- creating a comfortable setting with no interruptions

- issuing a written agenda
- preparing a written report of what was decided

Strategies

Some Possible Interview Strategies

- *Tell and sell.* You judge the person's performance and convey your opinion. You aim to persuade the person to adopt specific solutions for action:

Here's what I think about your work and I'd like you to try my suggestions for action.

- *Tell and listen.* You describe objectively the person's performance but say nothing further. You listen carefully to what the other person says about it:

I'll explain how I see your work, after that it's up to you to say what you think.

- *Joint problem solving.* You jointly review performance focusing not on the individual but on the entire work situation. Together you identify actions:

We'll discuss work problems and possible solutions; together we'll work out what to do.

- *Self appraisal.* You prompt the other person to give a personal audit in which they identify strengths and development needs. The person offers suggestions for change and you add your ideas:

You tell me how effective you are being, I trust you'll be much tougher on yourself than I'd ever be; I'll add my thoughts on further action to yours.

- *Goal Setting.* Separately and together you define the person's future objectives and how their performance will be assessed against these aims. Any agreed actions are concerned with achieving the aims:

We'll set some mutually acceptable goals and decide how we'll monitor your progress; I'll suggest ways to help you achieve these goals.

Tips on Offering Adverse Comments on Performance

Volunteering. Encourage the person to volunteer the information first. For example, ask them to identify their current strengths and development needs.

Sandwiching. Sandwich critical comments between encouragement and supportive remarks. For example, you might say, 'What I particularly admire about you is how you will always work late when necessary. I am less admiring though about your timekeeping in the mornings. What do you think you could do about this?'

Pre-meeting work. Before an appraisal ask the person to complete an appraisal preparation form to identify areas of strength and weakness.

Sharing incidents. Describe adverse incidents objectively and explain their known consequences. Ask the person for their comments for future actions by both the company and the individual.

Sharing the blame. When someone has not performed well it is partly your responsibility – perhaps they did not know what was expected, misunderstood instructions, were inadequately trained, had insufficient resources and so on. Be prepared to accept some of the responsibility for the other person's performance.

Thomas Watson, one of the founders of IBM, once called into his office an executive who had recently lost the company $10 million. 'Do you know why you're here?' asked Watson.

'I suppose you are going to fire me,' replied the anxious manager.

'Fire you? are you crazy? I've just spent $10 million on your education.'

Unpalatable truths For some managers appraisals are a longed for opportunity to dole out some criticism for past behaviour. While the meeting is certainly a chance for some home truths, it is seldom effective to deliver these in a spirit of punishment and revenge.

Without pulling your punches, take care how you deliver criticism and unpalatable facts. (see Chapter 11 on problem people). Always assume someone wants to do a good job.

If you criticise, do so with kindness, offering specific examples, not generalities.

● The secret of giving adverse feedback is offering it with care and respect.

Rather than talking about what kind of person they are, focus on behaviour and what they have done. Never cast doubts on someone's motives or their integrity unless you have absolute proof, and even then think whether this will really achieve your purpose. Also, avoid apologising for giving adverse feedback. The other person is entitled to know when they are not meeting your expectations.

Listening   Active listening is essential in any appraisal encounter.

● Use body language to express attention and interest.

● Avoid hasty judgements.

● Do not interrupt

● Feed back information to show it has been heard properly.

● Encourage the other person to do most of the talking.

● Use occasional silences to prompt more responses.

If you speak for more than about a fifth of the time, this is not appraisal, it is lecturing. Reflect back to the other person your interpretation of what they are saying and feeling. Feelings are an important part of the experience and you need to carefully tap into what the other person is experiencing. Conclude the meeting with a brief summary and check that the other person agrees with it.

Ensure that the event concludes on a positive note with the person feeling up rather than down. You halve the chances of improvement if they depart in a state of gloom.

Follow up

After the appraisal meeting either you or the appraisee should complete a report showing:

● the original purpose of the meeting

● the points discussed

- conclusions reached
- objectives set
- training and development actions required
- matters left unresolved.

Both parties should agree the contents with enough space to add comments. Parts of the report may need to be kept confidential, for example when there are issues of promotion or career changes. Keep such items to a minimum, as secrecy does not build trust.

Follow through

The other person will be more committed to pursuing a goal, making a change or behaving differently if you show that you take the appraisal seriously. For example, if during the appraisal you agreed to undertake an action, complete your side of the bargain.

Consider asking the other person to comment on the experience to you or to an independent third party. This will help you develop your own appraisal technique.

Team appraisal

An emerging trend is the move from appraising individual performance towards assessing the performance of an entire team. The impact of team appraisals can be considerable. However, these sessions are no substitute for meeting with each team member to review their work performance.

In an effective team appraisal system, all members comment on the group's performance and sometimes on each other's contribution. For example, the team may offer their collective views on the effectiveness of the current leader. This kind of appraisal needs to be handled with care. It may be sensible to start such a process with an outside specialist's help.

Further reading

FLETCHER C. *Appraisal: Routes to improved performance*. London, IPM, 1993

HUNT N. *How to Conduct Staff Appraisals*. Plymouth, How To Books, 1994

4 *four*

Coaching

Brian is a carpet expert. He knows all about materials, measuring, fitting, and laying. But his job at the RoomService Design company in Chessington is demanding. He therefore wants his small staff to improve their skills so that they too can handle almost any carpet project.

Brian needs to learn to coach, to pass on his knowledge for the benefit of the customers, the staff and himself. Yet he is unsure what is involved in coaching and how to do it well.

Coaching is built into every manager's job, although not always explicitly. Every day supervisors, managers, team leaders coach their colleagues, helping them to be more effective.

Coaching brings out the best in people. It is often seen as giving instruction or demonstrating a particular skill to the 'trainee'. The latter then has a go and receives feedback on their performance. However, the role of managers has been shifting towards supporting rather than controlling. Coaching based mainly on instruction is the old approach. While it may have its place, it is now part of a wider process.

You need to view coaching in the wider context of the organisation's longer term future. It is not merely a tool to help someone improve, it is a way of developing the full potential of employees. These are the people who will determine whether or not the organisation has a future in the first place.

Coaching is consequently a strategic tool for ensuring that the organisation has the capabilities required for living in the future it intends to create. It is also how experienced, visionary managers pass on their knowledge and enthusiasms. In essence it is an empowering tool and a vital link between learning and doing.

Coaching

Coaching means systematically helping people develop skills, competencies or understanding, through guided practical experiences and regular feedback. It means enlisting people's involvement and supporting their learning and development. It differs from:

- *training*, as it may not use practical experience and feedback
- *counselling*, because it is not a process for overcoming a specific situation or problem; unlike counselling which starts with the past, coaching is focused immediately on opportunities in the future
- *mentoring*, because it is not focused primarily on career planning
- *appraisal*, because it is usually an informal process and is done more frequently than a few times a year.

Coaching is a continuous process and skilled managers constantly look for opportunities to do it. Often these are spontaneous rather than planned. What makes coaching special is your relationship with the person being coached. The ideal session is really a conversation between equals, one of whom happens to have more knowledge or skill.

Management coaching involves you doing most of the talking and offering skills, knowledge and experience. You help someone solve a problem or carry out a task better.

Achievement coaching involves you doing most of the listening. You focus on unlocking the person's potential, gaining their commitment, developing their expertise. It's an ongoing process of providing the opportunity and encouragement for the person to address their particular needs and personal objectives. If you concentrate on achievement coaching you do not need expert knowledge about a subject. After all, many successful Wimbledon coaches have themselves never actually won the tennis trophy.

You cannot force someone to be coached, they have to want to take part. Effective coaches:

- get satisfaction from the success of others
- give time to the coaching role.

The biggest block to effective coaching is insufficient time. You will almost certainly have to rearrange your priorities, but it will ultimately save you time.

Benefits of coaching

Unlike formal instruction or supervision, coaching lets you learn too. The benefits include:

- developing leadership skills
- giving people a chance to contribute their ideas
- generating real work, while learning
- enhancing the skill and competency of the coach and the learner
- forcing a focus on quality
- high ownership and commitment.

Coaching Roles

Appraiser:	agrees what development is needed and a plan for getting there; observes and assesses
Supporter:	creates opportunities for learning; provides support, services and resources; develops positive relationships
Communicator:	gives balanced and constructive feedback; counsels; offers advice and suggestions; is clear and informative
Motivator:	challenges and has expectations; encourages; gives recognition; helps the learner take responsibility; understands.

Skills

Managers who demand high levels of control seldom make good coaches and tend to reduce a sense of ownership about the learning. The ideal approach is one of sharing. To be an effective coach you need to create situations that link the work to the coaching. Your own management style, priorities and attitudes also heavily influence how people respond to you as a coach.

'We simply cannot afford the luxury of managing people in the same way as we have in the past. All managers have had to become more of a coach and counsellor, leaders who are receptive to the notion of empowerment.' Stephen Croni, Group Personnel Director, Rank Xerox

To adapt your approach to different people means listening to what help they want:

- recognising opportunities to gain experience
- reflecting on their personal development and performance
- developing clear ideas and guidelines about what to do
- experimenting with new skills and methods.

The coaching sequence

The essence of coaching is:

- understanding
- practice
- feedback.

For this you need to:

- prepare
- meet
- follow up.

Step 1: establish current competence

Establish a clear base line from which to start coaching by discovering what the person knows about the subject. Often you will be surprised by their knowledge. Poor coaches plough ahead regardless, causing boredom or frustration.

Make the coaching environment as pleasant as possible and stop incoming phone calls and interruptions.

Let the learner describe their current skill level in their own words. Offer open questions ('Tell me about . . .') that encourage them to expound on what they know. During this time, listen actively, without making judgements. This is no time to criticise the person's ability or to boast about your own skills. Concentrate instead on clarifying what exactly the person knows, can do and might want to learn.

Step 2: agree learning objectives

Ask the learner to define their own development aims. You cannot readily impose learning objectives on someone else, so encourage the person to take ownership of the learning process. You cannot for example, learn to ride a bicycle or learn to play drop shots at tennis for someone else. They must commit to the learning themselves, with your help and encouragement.

Explain how the coaching will work and set a standard for the person to achieve. Treat the discussion of what is to be learned as a partnership, in which you both work together to define the agreed outcome. Once this has been determined summarise the learning objectives, if necessary in writing. Finally, avoid discussing learning objectives as if you are dealing with faulty behaviour.

Achievement coaching questions

- How do you see yourself achieving that?
- What would you like to do?
- When do you think you will complete that?
- How do you see that working?
- What resources will you need?
- Who else will be working with you on this?
- How could you do that better next time?
- What would success look like?
- How could you make that happen?
- Where do you plan to do this?
- What are the choices facing you?

Step 3: create hands-on opportunities

To be an effective coach you must keep creating opportunities for the person to learn through actually doing. Offer hands-on opportunities where the person knows what authority they have to act and that they are free to make mistakes. It may require ingenuity on your part to create such an environment.

Remind the learner that you are available to help if needed and clarify when the next coaching situation will occur. Finally, before letting the learner loose to experiment, ask for any worries or concerns they may have about the hands-on experience. Deal with these issues sensitively, even if you feel they are groundless.

Share what works for you without saying, 'This is the right way'. Sometimes the person will later devise an even better way of doing something. Many great new ideas have come from learners who never realised there was a so-called 'right way'.

Once you have set up a live hands-on situation, avoid overloading the learner with constant advice. Let them get on with it and learn through making their own mistakes.

Step 4: give feedback

Good coaches offer plenty of praise and encouragement. Use open and probing questions ('What did you discover from doing it that way?') without conducting a cross-examination. Be a mirror rather than a critic.

Encourage the learner to try again, perhaps offering a few tips. Rather than demand wholesale changes ('You're going to have to do it entirely differently.') suggest an adjustment before the learner goes off to try again.

Avoid words like 'wrong', 'bad', 'incorrect'. Instead make room for the person to assess themselves. Ask questions rather than pass judgement. Refrain from showing the person entirely what to do, instead encourage a return to another hands-on attempt.

Step 5: recap and summarise

Constantly recap, summarising learning points and what has been agreed in the way of action. Use questions to prompt discussion about progress and check the learner's understanding. Give praise while looking for more good points to reinforce.

10 coaching tips from those on the receiving end

- Treat me as a person in my own right.
- Set me a good example.
- Encourage and support me.
- Praise me when I do well.
- Back me up with your superiors.
- Do your own job competently.
- Do not pull rank on me.
- Keep me informed about what I need to know.
- Take time from your normal duties to coach me.
- Never under-estimate what I can do.

Unwilling learners

Not everyone takes kindly to being coached. It may require considerable tact and perseverance to help them accept help. Whether someone is willing to be coached may depend on the approach you adopt with them. For example, if you push hard, confront, challenge and criticise, you may simply generate resistance.

> It is the willingness of people to give and receive coaching, to help others to learn and be ready to learn themselves, that will create the context in which effective leadership can flourish.
>
> Geoff Keeys, Director of Personnel and Business Services, Prudential Corporation plc

By staying cool and dispassionate as a coach, you may help learners to think things through for themselves. Yet if you are too distant you may be regarded as impersonal and uncaring. Similarly, an overenthusiastic coach can motivate through excitement and energy, yet may be seen by some people as intimidating.

Be willing to experiment with your coaching style.

Further reading

KALINAUCKAS P. and KING H. *Coaching: Realising the potential.* London, IPD, 1994

5 *five*

Negotiating

Every manager negotiates, through:

- informal bargaining
- formal bargaining with trade unions and other bodies
- commercial bargaining.

Bargaining is a polite word for haggling. People do it in bazaars and in multinational trading corporations. You cannot avoid it in your job if you are to be effective.

Informal bargaining occurs so often we hardly think twice about it. For example, when you ask a colleague to complete a report by mid-week and they suggest that the end of the week would be preferable, you are negotiating.

Formal negotiating usually involves a trade union or other representative body. While it may be perfectly amicable, it may still involve hard bargaining. It might encompass wide-ranging issues such as annual pay agreements, working practices or introducing new technology.

Commercial bargaining is about making business deals. For example, negotiating a new contract with a supplier, completing an important sale, agreeing a takeover, all involve commercial bargaining skills.

Negotiating skills

- a quick mind
- a strong reserve of patience
- an ability to conceal without lying
- a capacity to inspire trust
- assertiveness at key moments and self-effacement at other times

- a knowledge of the issue, combined with an ability to see the broader picture.

You are a negotiator by virtue of your management role. Even if you delegate the job to an expert at bargaining, you can seldom escape the need to become involved in issues such as power, strategy, tactics and fallback positions.

What you negotiate for is even more important than how you negotiate. There is no point in doing it brilliantly if you are negotiating for the wrong things. Successful managers negotiate in the wider context of the organisation's strategic intent. They bargain in order to build the future.

Power

Power underpins all bargaining and is the factor that determines the final result. Bargaining power is:

- the strength of the negotiator's position, once all bluffing has ended.

There is no real bargaining when one side holds overwhelming power. It only begins to matter at the margin, where both sides believe they can obtain something of what they what.

Because bargaining mainly occurs when there is a slight imbalance of power, there is a tendency for each party to try to minimise the disadvantages facing them, instead of maximising their gains. By attempting to do both simultaneously you may not optimise the final outcome.

Bargaining power reflects several unknowns:

- My bargaining power is based on the losses you would suffer if you were to agree or disagree with my proposal.
- Your bargaining power is based on the losses I would suffer if I were to agree or disagree with your proposals.

Bargaining Power can be:

- understood sufficiently to use it to help you achieve your aims
- approximately calculated
- applied to the bargaining situation
- analysed for its constituents and how these are distributed between the parties
- used to formulate a strategy.

Despite the unknowns you can still improve your ability to negotiate by analysing your bargaining power. Many managers resist the opportunity to do this, preferring to rely solely on instincts. They plunge straight into negotiations and test out the reality of their bargaining power. Generally that is a weak negotiating approach, so spend time assessing your bargaining power before starting any actual negotiations. For example, strengthen your position by basing it on facts, rather than speculation or wishful thinking.

Assessing your bargaining power helps formulate your aims and strategy. You will then bargain with more confidence.

Conflict versus co-operation

At some level all negotiating is about resolving conflict. Sometimes the conflict is in the open. Everyone involved knows it exists and the main issue is how to resolve it satisfactorily. Occasionally the conflict is hidden or beneath the surface of the discussions. No one alludes to it, yet it exists.

It is also helpful if you realise that there are three main possible outcomes:

- One party gains and the other loses – win/lose.
- Both parties gain a mutual benefit – win/win.
- Both parties gain no benefit – lose/lose.

In some commercial negotiations the aim may be to achieve gains at the other party's expense. Similarly, there are situations where the best way to achieve what you want is to aim for a result where both parties feel they are gaining something worthwhile. The win/lose variety tends to be fairly common, particularly when dealing with trade unions or those who have relatively less power than you, but it is not necessarily the ideal result.

In commercial bargaining or informal negotiations between departments and divisions, or between you and individuals, both sides may need to emerge with a sense of victory.

Establishing whether a situation has a substantial built in conflict

- State the issue about which you will be negotiating.
- List the points you and the other party will be most likely to raise about the issue.
- For each point, state the most likely settlement that you and the other party will try to achieve.

- If the issues or the outcomes that each side wants do not substantially coincide, then bargaining is likely be one based on win/lose

The traditional view of negotiation is confrontational, in which win/lose is inevitable. Nowadays, however it is increasingly seen in more human terms. Thus in win/win situations you do not move rapidly to litigation, to crucifying your opponent or humiliating the other person. Instead you seek to avoid stalemate and achieve fairness.

The stages of negotiation

Most bargaining involves:

- preparing
- putting your offer on the table
- clarifying
- negotiating
- closing
- implementation.

Preparing

If there is a great deal at stake, preparation is essential. In too many situations managers fail to prepare in depth, and find themselves facing opponents who have done their homework. Few trained trade union representatives for example, would dream of starting serious negotiations without considerable preparation and research such as:

- systematically analysing what may arise during bargaining
- assessing bargaining strengths
- determining which outcomes are essential and which merely desirable.

Develop a clear idea about the territory over which the negotiations may range. There is nothing more annoying than to enter a negotiating situation thinking the issues you will talk about are of one kind, only to discover the other party has a long list of others they intend to raise.

- What issues is the other party likely to raise?
- What information do you need to deal with these issues?
- What is your intended response to these issues?

Decide in advance what is and is not negotiable. When you have determined your 'bottom line' you become more clear about how you might proceed. For example, you may decide that there is some level of pay increase above which you are not prepared to go. This is your non-negotiable position. Once you know this you can consider different ways to approach the negotiations.

Your preparations should include deciding what will be your highest and lowest demands. What concessions are you prepared to make and what are the largest and smallest ones?

The formal preparatory steps

- Define your negotiating aim – the settlement you want.
- Clarify your bargaining power compared to the other side's.
- Prior to bargaining strengthen your power, or weaken the other side's.
- Devise detailed bargaining points to achieve your overall aim.
- Prepare your case and carefully document it.
- Fully brief your bargaining team.
- Clarify the limits of authority for those negotiating on your behalf.

Putting your offer on the table

This is when you state your position confidently and clearly. You broadly explain what you want, without offering many specifics. If you need to seek information at this stage, ask open questions that require more than a yes or a no. You may never need to put your full offer on the table. Often you can let it emerge naturally as the negotiations progress.

It is usually best to present your initial offer as a basis for discussion rather than a 'take it or leave it' statement. Any experienced trade union negotiator, for example, will simply respond to it as a negotiating tactic.

Clarifying

Any offer will almost certainly need further clarification. Having listened to the other party's aims, clarify the situation by summarising the main aims of both parties. Obtain an agreement that your summary is correct.

You may need clarification on issues such as timescale, the meaning of certain terms, the scale of charges, the implications of an event such as a cancellation of an order halfway through a contract, and so on.

Negotiating

Although, each bargaining situation is unique, the general negotiating process is similar in all situations.

Some possible bargaining ground rules

- We have previously bargained about an issue, so we can do so now.
- We adhere to what we agree.
- There is a deadline for completing our negotiations.
- Sanctions imposed before the negotiating deadline are disruptive.
- There is room for manoeuvre in both parties' position.

An important assumption underpinning most negotiations is that both parties are prepared to some extent to alter their position. So you need to decide in advance your:

- ideal settlement
- acceptable settlement
- minimum fallback position.

The *ideal settlement* is what you obtain when the negotiations achieve everything you wanted and maybe more. An *acceptable settlement* is one you are prepared to live with. It gives you a great deal of what you hoped for but not everything. It is acceptable because the costs of trying to achieve still more would be too high. Your *minimum fallback position* is the one you must achieve; otherwise you leave the negotiating table. A typical fallback position is the minimum price for which you are prepared to sell your product or service when negotiating with a potential customer.

Closing

Now is the time to summarise the discussed proposals and to ask: 'Have we got a deal?' Avoid final tactics of the 'take it or leave it' kind. This merely gives the other party the chance to say, 'I'll leave it then', and all the negotiating is wasted.

When summarising, be sure the other party keeps nodding as you list the areas of agreement. If you detect any hesitation, stop and check again that you have agreement.

In closing, confirm that you will be producing your own notes of the agreement and will be circulating them.

Strategy Your bargaining strategy is the broad plan for obtaining what you want. You achieve this by using a variety of bargaining tactics. Strategy alters according to each situation and you need a flexible approach.

Your negotiating strategy will depend on your bargaining strength, your relationship with the other party and other constraints, such as conventions. It can be either *offensive* or *defensive*. A win/lose approach is an offensive strategy, while adopting a win/win approach is a more defensive one.

A win/win strategy works if the other party has a similar approach, or can be persuaded to adopt one. However, if the other party is operating entirely in a win/lose mode, it may be harder to reach a final outcome.

Starting negotiations with a win/win approach is generally more effective since, if necessary, you can usually revert to a win/lose one later. You cannot easily revert back to a win/win strategy, since there may be too many barriers of trust to overcome.

Since no single strategy works for all occasions you should be alert to

- opening moves
- increases in bargaining power
- sanctions.

Opening moves are an important part of effective negotiations. They set the pattern for all future discussions. For example, suppose one of your opening moves is to insist that the negotiations exclude any discussion about future redundancies. Once the other party has agreed, it may prevent them raising all kinds of issues that you do not want to debate. Pitch your opening bid too high and you risk driving the other party from the negotiating table. Set your opening move too low and it will be difficult to achieve a settlement above this later. Generally, however, a high demand has advantages over a low one. You will know that your opening bid is too low if the other party immediately accepts it, without question, but this may not matter if you have decided in advance what your minimum requirements are.

Increasing your bargaining power is not an end in itself. It usually occurs because neither party feels able to get what they want.

Ways of increasing your bargaining power

- Try to determine the agenda, for example by excluding or including certain issues.
- Recruit an ally.
- Obtain important new information.
- Gain some kind of leverage over the other party.
- Delay negotiations until you improve your position.
- Initiate action in another area which raises the costs to the other party

of disagreeing with your offer.

● Link the current issue with other ones that may not initially seem significant yet later become critical.

● Weaken the other party's position in some way.

Consider whether you are doing everything possible to maximise your position. Should you for instance refrain from some action that you are currently taking? Can you force the other party to take some action not currently being taken? This is not to say that it always pays to try and increase your bargaining power. If you are dealing with people who report to you, for example, they are likely to feel you have quite enough power already.

Sanctions are ways to punish the other party and you can use them either before or during negotiations. They are usually adopted to drastically alter your current bargaining position.

An example of a sanction occurs when you say you will not negotiate unless people first return to work. A more drastic one is threating to lock employees out unless they first return to work. A typical sanction in commercial negotiations is to warn the other party that the price will rise if negotiations cannot be concluded by a certain date, or the order is not of a sufficient size.

Sanctions are manipulative and can quickly antagonise the other party to the detriment of the final settlement. However, they show that you really mean business and affirm your bargaining position.

Tactics   Tactics are the means by which you try to achieve your negotiating plan. While there are literally hundreds of different tactics, two important ones are:

● Assume everything is negotiable.

● Never make a concession without receiving one in return.

Take it for granted that ultimately everything is negotiable. No matter how strongly the other party asserts their position, you should always assume that at some price, or with some concession, they can be persuaded to do what you want. You may not know the price of the final settlement, but assuming that everything can be negotiated encourages you to tackle the bargaining confidently and to keep looking for opportunities to reach a conclusion.

Since most negotiations consist of concessions by both parties another basic tactic is never to give away anything without obtaining something in return. For example, when negotiating with a customer who demands a discount, you might concede one only for a large order. What you get in return may not necessarily be entirely tangible. It might for example be goodwill or renewed motivation. For example, your response to a subordinate who asks for an extra day off might be to demand that they complete a report before leaving.

Use a particular tactic because you expect it to achieve a certain specific result at the time. For instance, do not throw away a request for an adjournment by saying something like 'Let's have coffee.' Adjournments are particularly useful for buying time while you consider an issue, or taking the pressure off you or your negotiating team. Requesting an adjournment is also a useful way of encouraging your opponent to spend time considering whether to accept your point of view, without them losing face.

Some well-known negotiating tactics

- In the early stages, conceal as much information about your own position as you think sensible.

- Try redefining how the other party sees its own position so as to help it shift towards your own position.

- Undermine the arguments of the other party by: challenging assumptions; disputing facts; attacking conclusions; pointing to inconsistencies.

- Reduce the other party's credibility by: questioning their experience; suggesting that they are losing control; negotiating to the point of their mental exhaustion.

- Strengthen your own arguments and credibility by: demonstrating a mastery of detail; making an appeal to reason or emotion; minimising your weaknesses by claiming the point has already been taken into account.

- Encourage movement by the other party in their position by: summarising the negotiations so far, suggesting it is time for mutual concessions; suggesting a new position which represents a different point of departure for both parties; linking two or more issues to help get nearer a settlement; suggesting an adjournment while indicating that during it you want the other party to pay attention to a certain issue.

- Enable the other party to abandon a previous commitment by: describing all the concessions you have made so far; suggesting that circumstances have changed; blaming some other party or situation for the present situation – for example the government, another union, competitive pressures; suggesting that there has been a misunderstanding; referring the whole matter for resolution to another individual or group – for example asking ACAS, the government arbitration service, to help reach a settlement.

- Attempt to move towards a settlement. Be alert for ways of bringing matters to a conclusion, choosing a moment when events are going well.

- In reaching a settlement, ask the other party to re-state it in their own words.

- Agree ways to monitor that the settlement is being implemented as intended.

- Finalise and document the agreement.

Implementation

There is considerable scope for misunderstanding about what has or has not been agreed. So all the negotiations should be properly documented. During the discussion stages always verbally summarise any concessions you are making while omitting those offered by the other party. However, ensure the other party's concessions are properly noted in the documentation.

It is sometimes said that whoever keeps the minutes of a meeting holds the real power and in negotiating situations this can certainly be true. With complicated negotiations it may be hard to remember every concession and every figure agreed. If the other party fails to make careful notes, yours may be the ones that ultimately determine the final arrangements.

Successful negotiations mean some agreed action, or even inaction.

- A trade union agrees to: adopt a new working practice; not to ban overtime; not go on strike.

- A customer agrees to: a contract; a price; a delivery time.

- A person reporting to you agrees to: behave in a new way; write a report; complete a project.

- Another department agrees to: produce a product; provide information; join a project team.

- You agree not to: take legal action in return for a supplier replacing faulty equipment.

Even if the other party does keep careful notes and circulates them after the bargaining session, make sure that you also circulate your own version. This helps retain your authority over the entire process.

When an agreement has been reached, the follow-through should involve both parties. Since many negotiations break down at the implementation stage, it is worth making a prior commitment jointly to monitor progress. This would include a further meeting shortly after implementation begins.

Joint monitoring of implementation allows a rapid response to any divergencies from what both parties are expecting from the negotiations. It also enables you jointly to agree some action.

Top 10 principles

- If you do not have to bargain, do not. If you can achieve what you want without making a concession do not offer one.

- Do your research. Discover as much as possible about your bargaining power and the other party's .

- Make the other side respond. Issuing an important demand early on and sticking to it forces the other party to work hard to obtain concessions .

- Initially, apply power gently. Only gradually let the message percolate through that you could do the other party harm, cause them problems, or offer benefits.

- Make them compete. Typically in sales negotiations, force the other party to try hard to get your attention, letting them know or think that they could lose out to someone else.

- Leave yourself room. Allow enough space to manoeuvre around the offer; initially ask for more than you expect and concede less than you would ultimately be willing to give.

- Maintain your integrity. Do not lie; if you make a commitment stick to it. If necessary be tough and abrasive, yet always trustworthy.

- Listen more than talk. Encourage the other party to reveal their information and position first; the more you listen the more you will learn about how to increase your bargaining power.

- Keep contact with their hopes. Stay in touch with the other's party's reactions and expectations; large demands need to be floated gently; there is a limit to how much you can demand without causing deadlock; watch for signs the other party is being pushed too far or fast.

● Let them get used to your big ideas. It may take time to come to terms with your demands; be patient and try not to settle too early.

Training

Negotiating is an art, not a science. Not everyone is a natural bargainer and you can obtain formal training in analysis, preparation and tactics.

Trade unions run extensive negotiating training sessions for their full time officials and it is therefore sensible for managers to also receive similar help. Practising bargaining and role playing is a useful way of learning off the job, and a typical programme may last around three days.

Further reading

FISHER R. and URY W. *Getting to Yes: Negotiating an agreement without giving way.* London, Business Books, 1991

KENNEDY G. *Everything is Negotiable.* London, Hutchinson Business Books, 1982.

6 *six*

Report Writing

The world is awash with management reports. It is almost like a disease. Many managers cannot resist producing them when often it would be better to make a live presentation.

Successful managers:

- know when a written report is the best solution
- understand what makes a report powerful.

A management report is directed at decision makers or those who can influence them. Most reports deal with an issue where there is usually a choice about what to do next.

In the wider context of the organisation's future, how you handle reports can help to set you apart from other managers with whom you are competing. By always placing your reports in the broader framework of the organisation's strategic intent, its aspirations and formal plans, you demonstrate a depth of thinking that will certainly make you special.

When to write a report

The first step, beyond seeing the task in the broader context, is to decide:

- whether a written report is required
- what kind of report is needed.

It is always worth checking whether a written report is absolutely essential. Often people ask for a report without giving any thought to what would be the most effective form of presentation. If you can make the presentation a live one this is nearly always preferable to a written report.

With the increased use of E-mail there is a natural pressure to expect reports to be in writing. But people soon learn to ignore E-mail so a physical document is usually preferable.

A written report freezes your views publicly, far more so than a verbal one. Once you have circulated a document it is not easy to retrieve it, amend it or take back conclusions or other possibly contentious facts.

Go for a written report when you cannot provide a personal presentation, or when you feel confident that what you want to say will stand up to reasonably close scrutiny.

How to write a report

Stages of Preparing a Report

Preparation

- identifying the issue
- terms of reference or report requirement
- information gathering
- analysis.

Production

- structuring
- writing, testing, revising, editing
- summarising
- physical production and distribution.

Follow through

- presentation
- further action.

Management reports that get full attention are:

- focused
- brief
- readable
- structured
- credible
- presentable
- accountable.

We will look at each in turn, to see how they can help you be more effective in your report writing.

Focused

It is not always immediately obvious who exactly will read a report. This may be so even when it is clear who has initially requested it – the sponsor. The latter may pass your material to others to make decisions. So it always pays to spend time checking out: 'Who else do you think may read my report?'

Have in mind a specific person for whom you are writing. Imagine talking to them and how you would explain what the material is all about. Directing the report at a specific person makes you more precise about your message. Even if the report is ultimately directed at a team, a board of directors or a committee, think of at least one important member to whom you can address your material.

Brief

Most reports are too long. Some companies restrict all reports to a single page of A4. This forces everyone to be incredibly clear about what they really want to say. However this is an extreme solution to what is essential a simple requirement:

● Keep the report brief enough to hold people's interest.

Brevity takes longer to achieve than a lengthy document because you must work at reducing inessential material. Brevity is obviously a matter of opinion, but a management report of more than half a dozen pages is usually too long.

To help achieve brevity, always start by listing the key points you want to make. A good discipline for all reports is to prepare a one page summary.

Most reports in fact fail not from lack of facts but from too many. You are preparing a management report, not an encyclopedia. Keep asking: 'Is this fact or statement really essential?'

Readable

If you have focused your report you are well on the way to making it readable. Readability is not just a subjective matter of whether someone likes what they see. It is a measurable indicator that the report is likely to be understood by the audience concerned.

Readable reports

● Keep opening paragraphs clear, short and relevant.
● Pose issues concisely so that potential readers will understand them.

- Offer decisions or proposals in a neutral, thoughtful manner.
- Use short sentences of under 25 words.
- Test the report on a 'guinea pig' to discover any faults.
- Avoid jargon even if readers understand it.
- Use language rather than underlinings to express emphasis.

Many of the better word processors now include an automatic check on readability. There are also separate readability products that analyse your reports in even more detail. Stylewriter by Editor Software (for example) works with many word processors and provides some wide ranging information such as:

- jargon
- clichés
- redundancies, tautologies
- overwriting
- sexist words
- passive verbs
- hidden verbs
- misused words
- grammatical faults.

Given the ease with which reports can now be thoroughly checked there is little excuse for not doing so.

Structured

Management reports need a definite structure. Although different reports may require different structures a useful one is:

- management summary (1-2 pages)
- introduction
- background to report
- body of report, including analysis
- conclusions
- recommendation
- appendix.

In a lengthy report these sections will be physically separated from each other by headings, separate pages, different coloured paper and so on. Put low priority material in appendices or in a separate supporting document.

A proper structure means that sentences, paragraphs and sections fit logically together. For example:

- Does each new paragraph flow logically from the previous one, or does it move to a new topic without warning?
- Is there adequate supporting information?
- Do recommendations (or decisions) logically follow from the analysis?

At the start of a long report explain its structure, as this helps the reader understand the logical flow and makes them more willing to wait for certain information to be presented. For example, you may say: 'This report concludes with 25 recommendations for further action.'

Credible

Credibility stems from:

- sufficient factual evidence
- analysis supporting conclusions
- explaining the reliability of the evidence
- stating what value judgements and preferences are used
- fully thinking through the likely consequences of recommendations
- consistency
- overall presentation.

Lack of any of these will rapidly consign your report to the bin or a dusty shelf.

There is no such thing as an objective fact. The decision to include or exclude information implies judgement and bias.

Numbers Where possible quantify information and present conclusions, recommendations and decisions in a numerate way. Numbers help people understand the importance of issues.

However, masses of figures are not necessarily convincing; they often merely confuse. For example, will providing numbers to several decimal places really enhance the report, or will it just sow seeds of confusion?

If you are a 'numbers' person and have worked hard to produce data, it may be painful to consign much of the hard won facts to an appendix. Yet this may be the best way to help the reader.

If you cannot face checking all the numbers for accuracy, ask someone else to do it – but do it. For example, columns and rows should tally and formulae need to be the right ones and free from typing errors or arithmetical slips.

Limit the number of figures you put in a table or series of columns. Be sure that any tables of figures show clear patterns or messages that the reader cannot readily miss.

Where possible, rank numbers from highest to lowest, from most important to least important, from most topical to most dated and so on. Rankings improve clarity and help the reader to see patterns.

Presentable

This element covers a large territory and includes:

- general appearance
- numbering systems
- graphics.

General appearance If the report is worth writing, it is worth presenting with impact. So ensure that the typing is well done and the printing is clear and easy to read. Are there any spelling mistakes, typographical errors, wrong numbers, punctuation disasters?

It may seem wrong to give a lot of attention to such apparently minor issues as how to make the front cover look interesting, or what would be an attentioin-grabbing title. But these can determine people's immediate reactions to a report.

If you present numerical tables, does each have a reference number and proper explanatory title? Is the layout of tables helpful? For example, vertical lines between columns of figures tend to prevent the eyes from moving across the page and absorbing the data as a whole.

Layout contributes to a good report. For example, use generous margins of at least an inch or more. Use plenty of white space and start different sections of the report on a fresh page. Consider whether the whole report will work better with double spacing.

Give thought to the type of binding used. Spiral binding allows pages to lie flat for easy reading, but it does not look particularly attractive. Thermal binding systems let pages lie flat while also looking neat.

The general appearance of the report should make the reader pick it up and think, perhaps unconsciously, 'This seems interesting or important, I'd better have a look.'

Numbering systems If you number your paragraphs keep the sequence simple. With the decimal method of paragraph identification you can use many levels. For example, in the first level you label paragraphs

1.1, 1.2, 1.3 and so on. In the second level, sub-paragraphs are labelled 1.1.1, 1.1.2, 1.1.3 and so on.

A third level makes it even more complicated, with figures such as 1.1.1.1; 1.1.1.2; 1.1.1.3 and so on. While this kind of numbering appeals to some people, it is generally not very helpful. A better approach is to:

- write the report with only three levels
- use a different notation for the different levels.

For example, having labelled your paragraphs 1.1; 1.2; 1.3 etc, for the next level adopt a notation such as:

    1.1

        (i)
        (ii)
        (iii)

If you must further subdivide, adopt yet another notation:

    1.2

        (i)
        (ii)
        (iii)

            (a)
            (b)
            (c)

But do you even need to label the second and third levels? Often by using a good desk top publishing programme or a top of the range word processor, you can merely identify the sub paragraphs through bullet points of different styles and indentations. For example:

    1.2

        ●
        ●
        ●

          ■
          ■
          ■

If you feel a two or three level structure is not detailed enough, remember that this is a management report. Rethink what you are saying and simplify it.

Graphics Graphics such as pictures, diagrams, charts and images, can convey your message with impact. But information is not automatically communicated well just because it is in graphical form.

Vary the graphics. Endless pie charts, for example, are not necessarily compelling to read. Also make sure that all graphics are:

- properly numbered
- titled
- neat
- professional-looking.

With presentation software so readily available, there is little excuse for presenting badly drawn graphics or amateurish looking charts. Programs such as Harvard Graphics are quick to learn, at least for producing basic visuals. However, be wary of over-reliance on computerised drawings. They may look rather soulless.

Impact To persuade senior management or others with resources, you need to anticipate their reactions. The chart below shows what to take into account.

Getting Your Proposals Accepted

- Show why the issue is important.
- Request resources for a short period of time.
- Accept variations in how proposals are implemented.
- Show why they will achieve a desired outcome.
- Explain why the proposals are an improvement.
- Present the proposals' superiority over others.
- Justify the costs.
- Demonstrate that the proposals can be evaluated easily.

Accountable

Take responsibility for interpreting information and offering conclusions, decisions or recommendations. It is not enough to write a management report with facts and information without making sense of the implications. Just presenting raw information is abdicating responsibility.

Inexperienced managers often feel uncomfortable with the need to be accountable for more than just presenting facts. They may believe it exposes them to being wrong, upsetting someone or even going beyond their remit. All three are possible. Yet to be a better manager you need to be prepared to run the risk.

A management report without conclusions or recommendations is unlikely to have any impact. It runs the risk of evoking the response from readers: 'So what?' Recipients of management reports want guidance on what to do; they want to hear what you think and what you believe should happen next. By implication, you know more about the issue than someone who has not written the report. No matter how many people contribute to a management report, it needs to show accountability by suggesting the next steps and their implications.

Keep proposals short and simple. Break down complicated ones into smaller suggestions that can be more readily grasped. The ultimate accountability test is when the reader of the report begins to ask: 'What is supposed to happen next?'

Further reading

LEIGH A. and MAYNARD M. 'Getting it Down' in *Perfect Communications.* London, Century Business, 1993

7 *seven*

Meetings

The chairman placed a £50 note on the table. With great deliberation he also put a large box of matches beside it. Next he removed a match and struck it. Holding the bank note he appalled everyone by setting fire to it. There was silence as people watched the money burn to a black cinder. 'That is how much we spend every five minutes in this room when we meet,' he announced to a stunned team. 'Let's try to use the time as productively as possible, shall we?' From then on meetings were conducted at a vigorous pace.

You do not have to burn £50 notes to make the point that meetings are expensive. You could just place a digital clock on the table, and represent the cost by counting from zero upwards.

Burning money and using digital clocks have both been used to remind people about the cost of meetings. However, effective meetings are vital for organisations to function properly.

In the wider context of the organisation's future, meetings matter a great deal, not just in the way they are conducted but in terms of the issues they address. As a manager you can play an important part in ensuring that meetings are focused on important organisational issues which relate to the future, not just the past.

As you call meetings, attend them or support them in some other way, keep asking:

- How will this gathering help the company thrive in the future?

Why meetings matter

The benefit of meetings

- They focus attention and feelings on what the organisation is all about.

- They involve people in decisions so that they are more likely to support them.
- They make people more accountable.
- They are a powerful way of persuading, analysing and being creative.
- They help unfreeze fixed ways of thinking and generate options.
- They are an important forum for selling proposals, justifying decisions and stopping unwanted actions.
- They help you gain power.

Meetings are a way for managers to enhance their power. When you act as a mediator, offer ideas, analyse and summarise, you have an impact both within the meeting and beyond it. You also enhance your power by choosing your meetings. Certain meetings can help build your image, enhance your personal network of contacts and demonstrate your leadership qualities.

The purposes of meetings

The meetings you attend will fall into certain clear categories, such as to:

- co-ordinate and control
- negotiate
- consult and inform
- solve problems and make decisions
- plan
- network.

Unproductive meetings usually occur because those attending are unclear about how to contribute. Make sure a conscious effort is made to clarify the reasons for getting together. Ask:

- What is the specific objective of the meeting?

Make it a habit at the start of each meeting to restate its purpose. Even if you are not chairing it, you will gain impact by suggesting that the chairperson does so.

With increasingly flatter hierarchies, and a growing emphasis on everyone in an organisation contributing creatively, there is a need for effective leadership of meetings. One person should generally take responsibility for how the meeting flows. Traditionally this is the chairing role. However the title is less important than having one person oiling the wheels of the meeting. Few gatherings of more than four or five people work well unless someone acts as facilitator or chairperson. Sometimes the role can be shared between several people.

Well-organised Meetings

- Someone leads, chairs or supports.
- Prompt starts.
- Focused discussion – people stick to the subject.
- Clear purpose or agenda.
- Agreed procedures.
- Time limited – usually a maximum of 90 minutes.
- Good preparation.
- Effort to reach conclusions via consensus.
- Discussion of relevant matters.
- Few interruptions.
- Everyone can contribute.
- Regular summarising.
- Good listening.
- End on time.
- Rapid publication of results and further action.

Good meetings are usually the result of planning, not chance. Take time to think about the nature of the meeting, who needs to be there, the duration, the contents and the location.

Get it clear in your mind what you want from each meeting and try to decide what the essential aspects are that must be covered. Take account of people's experience and what information they require to make a useful contribution. Consider also what questions they might want answered and prepare the right information for them. Also, consider how you will deal with people's reactions to a controversial subject. For example, will you allow plenty of time for people to express their feelings?

The agenda

There is considerable truth in the claim that whoever controls the agenda controls the meeting. It is certainly worth investing time getting the agenda right. Some of the basics of agenda planning are shown in the chart on page 62.

The Agenda

- Always have a written agenda if possible.
- Distribute the agenda well in advance.
- Tell the people the location, date, starting and finishing time.
- Encourage everyone to contribute to agenda creation.
- Agenda items should reach the agenda maker no later than three quarters of the way between one meeting and the next.
- Put easy items at the beginning, the harder items in the middle and end on an 'up' note.

Constructing an agenda is a definite art. Put the items in the wrong order, have too many of them, or too few, and the meeting can waste everyone's time. Packed agendas, for example, create undue pressure and discourage calm discussion. People may leave dissatisfied that the meeting has skirted over or missed items.

Start and finish with an item that involves everyone. People's energies will be higher in the middle or towards the start of the meeting than at the end. The bell-shaped agenda curve shown in the chart below is a useful guide for devising an effective agenda.

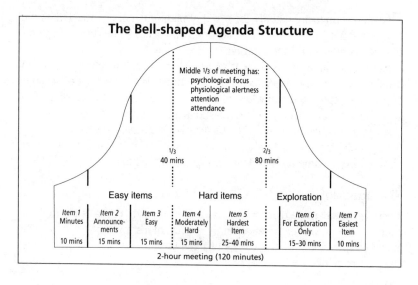

The Bell-shaped Agenda Structure

Middle ⅓ of meeting has:
psychological focus
physiological alertness
attention
attendance

⅓
40 mins

⅔
80 mins

Easy items			Hard items		Exploration	
Item 1 Minutes	Item 2 Announcements	Item 3 Easy	Item 4 Moderately Hard	Item 5 Hardest Item	Item 6 For Exploration Only	Item 7 Easiest Item
10 mins	15 mins	15 mins	15 mins	25–40 mins	15–30 mins	10 mins

2-hour meeting (120 minutes)

Participation

You will almost certainly want people in your meetings to contribute. Yet a common complaint by those who chair meetings is the difficulty of getting people to speak up. Large meetings are daunting. People are often reluctant to give their views, even if they feel quite strongly about them. Small meetings can also be difficult, with people feeling that every word they say will be put under the microscope.

Try breaking the meeting temporarily into smaller groups to discuss an issue for a few minutes and then ask for a response from each one. People often feel more comfortable reporting back what was said in a group than putting their own views on the line.

Consider asking people to come with a considered response to an issue and go systematically around the table seeking their comments. Check also for any feelings people may have about participating. You can encourage people to contribute by giving total attention to their contributions.

You will also encourage more participation by requiring everyone to express their objections and criticisms positively. Ask everyone to be alert for that familiar, negative phrase, 'Yes but . . .'

Ask people to summarise a previous person's contribution before making their own. This encourages listening, and people learn to build on each other's ideas. Summarising and rephrasing also helps participation, although doing it too often can be oppressive.

Issue the minutes of the meeting quickly as this reinforces what was agreed. This again emphasises your interest in what occurred and will make people feel valued.

Interruptions

Interruptions can seriously damage your meetings. The two main types you will have to deal with are internal and external.

Internal

Internal interruptions occur within the meeting itself. They are rather easier to anticipate, although not always easy to resolve. Watch for:

- people breaking off to make a phone call
- people shuffling papers noisily
- people talking during a presentation
- people using electronic pocket organisers, or lap-top computers
- people wandering around the room

- diversions
- late arrivals.

Neutralise all nearby phones by unplugging them or taking them off the hook. If someone says they must break off to make a call, challenge them directly. Ask if they can wait until the meeting breaks for coffee or ends. Tackle this sort of disruptive behaviour before it becomes too entrenched.

Shuffling of papers can irritate everyone, so listen for such distractions. At the start of the meeting ask people to handle papers quietly. Catch the eye of a noisy offender and press a forefinger to your lips while pointing at your own papers. If they still fail to get the message, say directly that you would appreciate it if people would keep the noise of paper movement to a minimum. You do not need to name the guilty person.

Talking during someone's presentation is a common problem. If you notice people starting to chat while someone else has the floor ask the chatterers if they are discussing anything important enough to share with the rest of the meeting. Or stop the meeting, saying, 'There appears to be a separate meeting going on.'

Some people love playing with their electronic gadgets and will do so if you allow them. Ask the meeting to agree a ground rule that the use of such gadgets is not acceptable, as it is distracting for others.

Wandering around the room is a more difficult interruption to counter since some people do it to release their creative energies. Constructive wanderers stay in touch with the meeting, nodding and looking interested. Destructive wanderers get up and sit down with little energy, move around aimlessly, opening windows, fiddling with objects.

Some people love to take a meeting off track. If you hold a regular meeting with the same people it is often worth discussing with them how everyone can help keep the meeting on course. For example, you could establish a group 'signal' that the discussion is veering off course.

Late arrivals are another common form of disruption . Tackle it early in the life of regular meetings. Make it clear that you want people to arrive on time and give a good example by being a good timekeeper yourself. If someone is a persistent late arrival, ask them privately if they have problems coming on time. It may be resolved by moving the meeting to a later time.

External

External interruptions to watch for include people with mobile pagers or phones, delivered messages and unexpected visitors, fire drills, noise from building work or other sources, and the arrival of refreshments.

Ask people to turn off mobile phones and pagers. For unexpected messages and visitors try posting a 'Please do not disturb' notice on the door. You may need to indicate what the person should do meanwhile, such as go to another contact point.

You probably cannot avoid random fire drills, but it is always worth checking whether there is likely to be one scheduled during your meeting.

There is nothing more distracting that someone barging into a meeting with a tray of drinks and setting them down noisily and proceeding to serve them. It is your meeting and you can decide on the domestic arrangements. Organise things so that refreshments arrive at a specified time, and plan the meeting accordingly.

The attenders

The kinds of people who may cause you difficulty in your meetings include:

- the obstructor
- the bore
- the comic
- the aspiring leader
- the bully
- the observer.

The *obstructor* keeps putting blocks in the way of progress. These can include constantly asking questions, challenging the veracity of information or demanding more facts. The obstructor is often adept at the 'Yes but . . .' technique. They often behave in this way because they fear that they have nothing of value to offer, so they end up attacking other people. They find lots of negative reasons why things cannot be done or will go wrong.

Turn these people to your advantage by directing their critical skills, asking them to follow up on detail, prepare a report and so on.

The *bore* likes the sound of their own voice, so leaves little room for anyone else's. They inflict their ideas or comments on the rest of the meeting, regardless of its immediate relevance. They talk a lot, repeat themselves and abuse valuable meeting time.

Deal with them by limiting their time slot. Intervene firmly when they have had their share. Try asking directly what the relevance is of the point they are making – although this may precipitate yet more verbiage. Ask pointedly, 'How does this move us forward?' or 'What solution are you proposing then?'

A technique for undermining both bores and obstructors is to write key decisions already made during a meeting on a flip chart. This stops them continuously returning to old territory, since others will soon say that the matter has already been dealt with.

Comics make jokes all the time, often at other people's expense. One initially enjoys their humour, until it starts to damage the meeting. Comics often use jokes as a form of defence, so that they will not be attacked. They are hard to handle because whatever you do can seem wrong. Not tackling them leaves the meeting at their mercy; tackling them can make you seem humourless.

Meetings without humour are dreary, but excessive humour stops serious ideas surfacing and prevents people expressing strong feelings in case they are ridiculed. Make it clear to your comic that while you really welcome humour it is wearing for everyone if it happens too often.

The *aspiring leader* keeps trying to do your job of chairing the meeting without your agreement. So, for example, they may persistently sum up and try closing down discussion prematurely.

Although leadership in meetings can often move around the table, aspiring leaders are seldom happy when other people start doing it too. Like comics, they are hard to deal with, since you want people to take responsibility and act assertively. The best tactic is to welcome their intervention but state clearly where you stand on the issue.

Bullies make others feel uncomfortable or humiliated. They are poor listeners and bulldoze their way in meetings. They are insensitive to feelings and usually excessively task-centred. Bullying can range from constantly interrupting people to hustling everyone to agree when they do not. Bullies rely on people not challenging them and if you do so, you will usually gain support from the rest of the meeting.

The *observer* never really participates, staying on the edge of the meeting the whole time. The classic observer ploy is to take extensive notes so that they appear to be too busy to make a contribution. Because they say so little, other people begin to feel that their silence is oppressive. When they do speak they often refuse to commit themselves or say what they really think about an issue.

Ask them to leave their extensive note taking till later, pointing out that you will issue minutes anyway. Perhaps even ask what the notes are about. You may discover to their embarrassment that the notes are totally unconnected with the actual meeting. Another tactic is to ask each person to comment on an issue and not let the observer off the hook. For example, you might say, 'I'd really appreciate knowing how you personally feel about this issue?' or 'Where exactly do you stand?'

Rewards

You can make or break a meeting by rewarding the wrong kind of behaviour. For example, if someone persistently arrives late and you stop the meeting to give them a full summary of the discussion, this may encourage them to continue being late.

If you start the meeting late to allow for late arrivals, you are punishing those who have arrived on time. Allow a strict margin of five minutes over the starting time and no more. Try asking people to arrive 10 minutes early and giving them something amusing or creative to do that they will enjoy, such as a puzzle or a problem to solve.

Reward those who have studied the papers in advance by thanking them and getting them to speak first. If someone says that they have not read the papers, ask them to listen to the discussion. There is nothing more infuriating and destructive than having the discussion dominated by those who have not got a proper grasp of the subject because they have failed to read the material provided.

If many people have not read the papers, suggest either that the item be delayed until another time or that the meeting spend a few minutes reading them.

Signs of failure

The danger signs that your meetings are failing may be many and varied. You need to be constantly alert for them and ready to take remedial action.

Signs that the meeting is failing:

- discussion dragging on interminably with no conclusions
- lack of participation
- many late arrivals
- the wrong people attend
- the meeting going too fast or too slowly
- excessive conflict
- bad interpersonal relations
- the meeting taking the wrong direction, such as cutting across existing organisational strategy
- no records are kept
- the person chairing becoming too involved and ceasing to be neutral.

If you are chairing the meeting people will expect you to take care of these matters.

Handling conflict

Some managers hate chairing meetings because they are expected to handle conflict. Many react by trying to suppress it, hoping that this will produce peace and constructive results. Often it achieves exactly the opposite result.

Meetings need to be safe places, where conflict can be handled appropriately, not eliminated. For instance, if your reaction to it is to become aggressive, you are unlikely to deal with it to the benefit of everyone else. The basic principle is to *allow conflict to occur*.

Having spotted a potential conflict situation, be positive and insist on the pros and cons being fully aired. Use a flip chart or white board divided down the centre and ask someone to list the arguments for and against. This focuses attention on facts rather than feelings.

Handling conflict also means dealing with the feelings, however, so try asking yourself these three questions:

- What does the speaker mean as opposed to what they are saying?
- What is the speaker feeling?
- What are the other people in the meeting feeling?

These questions can help you monitor what is happening and decide what to do next. For example, if someone is looking agitated or fuming with anger, indicate openly that you can see they are upset or concerned. Encourage them to share their feelings by suggesting that they state what exactly is worrying them. Steer the discussion away from attacking people in terms of personalities. Encourage people to clarify their disagreement with examples. Many conflicts vanish once you have detailed cases.

A classic way of dealing with conflict between two parties is to ask each to summarise the other's case to the latter's satisfaction.

You may face a choice between dealing with the conflict and completing the group task. Research suggests that a chairperson who concentrates almost solely on the task will seldom be particularly liked although they will probably be respected. The alternative role of smoothing ruffled feathers, and giving people support and encouragement, is one that wins you friends, but may ignore the importance of the task.

If you feel particularly torn by this dilemma, a useful solution is to ask someone else in the meeting to be responsible for oiling the wheels. This could mean taking a special interest on your behalf in watching for people who are feeling strongly about an issue and encouraging them to speak up. It might mean that they take responsibility for helping the meeting run to time.

Further reading

LEIGH A. and MAYNARD M. *Leading Your Team*. (Chapter Two). London, Nocholas Brealey 1995

8 *eight*

Decision Making

'Make every decision as if you owned the whole company,' suggested Robert Townsend, the renowned head of Avis. Wherever you are in the organisation, as a manager you will need to make decisions, and treating each as if it affected the entire enterprise is the way to act strategically.

Managers make decisions because they are constantly either responding to change or initiating it. A decision is only necessary if:

- there are two or more possible outcomes
- some value or importance is attached to the outcomes
- the actual outcomes differ in some way.

Decision making is fundamentally about choice. Without a choice you need make no decision. Similarly, if there is no real difference between the final outcomes, choosing hardly matters either.

In the wider context of the organisation's future, your managerial decision making is a way for you to excel, to stand out from those with whom you are competing. When you understand your organisation's strategic intent, what it aspires to be, you can place all decisions in a powerful perspective.

Review your decisions in terms of where the organisation is going. How will the decision help this journey? By attempting to think strategically about decision making you signal that you see your role as leading, not merely managing.

You could think of a decision as the moment of making a final choice. Yet this is only part of choosing. By only seeing decision making as an event, a single point in time, you risk missing other important steps. It is a process, not an event.

- All circumstances surrounding a choice encompass decision making.

Outcomes

One way to improve your decision making is to list and analyse the likely outcomes systematically. Experienced managers often devise a table showing the various outcomes under different circumstances.

Suppose you want to decide whether or not to raise the prices of your product. You may consider two important possibilities: increasing the prices by different amounts, and the reaction of competitors. The payoff table below summarises some potental outcomes:

		Own Price Rises		
		Small	Medium	Large
Competitor Reaction	No response	Result 1	Result 2	Result 3
	Matched response	Result 4	Result 5	Result 6
	Reduction	Result 7	Result 8	Result 9

Potentially, all decisions could be fitted into a table along these lines. In practice, only certain ones justify the effort. Some choices, for example, are too simple to make it worth while, others are too complex to handle in this way.

When you finally make a choice, you will want to feel that it is the best possible one in the circumstances. However, you may need to define just what you mean by 'best'. For example, a narrow view of profits might exclude any concern for the environment. Yet ignoring environmental concerns may ultimately damage the company's reputation and ability to retain its existing customers.

Decision making deals with the impact of events in the future, which is never absolutely predictable. So two basic components of all decisions are:

● uncertainty

● risk.

Uncertainty implies unknown outcomes. We cannot know all the possible outcomes of a potential decision. For example, you may never be able to unravel all the possible consequences for the company of the dismissal of an employee.

Uncertainty over the outcome is why some people find decision making stressful. One can minimise the uncertainty by, for example, attempting to analyse all the outcomes, maximising the amount of information available at the point of choice, or avoiding decisions where the degree of uncertainty is simply unacceptable.

Risk analysis

In formal decision making, risk has a more precise meaning than uncertainty. It is about the *degree* of uncertainty. Rather than saying the outcome is uncertain, we quantify the nature of this uncertainty.

Risk estimates are based on measurements, an intuitive guess about the chances of something happening, or a mixture of both. Decision experts call this risk analysis. Risk analysis is a structured approach to making choices. It usually involves calculations using systematically collected information. For example, when a company accepts a quality standard of one faulty component in 10,000, this is usually determined from detailed information about past failures and any new systems installed to prevent them occurring.

Risk analysis is a highly numerate discipline, involving applied mathematics and statistical techniques. Using these, risk analysts try to reduce the level of uncertainty attached to the final choice.

Most busy managers do not have time to become experts in risk analysis. However, you need to be aware that such a discipline exists, that there are people trained in methods of calculating risk, and when it might be worth using such specialised support.

The decision process

You can enhance your own decision making by adopting a systematic approach to making choices. You can still use your intuition and natural judgement, but you supplement them with formal analysis to throw more light on the likely outcomes.

You can start by adopting a framework for handling the decision process. A framework does not ensure that you take effective decisions, nor does it make the final choice easier. However it does enable you to tackle the task thoroughly and generate more knowledge about the possible consequences and the risks.

A decision framework can:

- ensure that you include all important steps in making a choice
- provide a way of judging the choices
- help explain your choices to other people
- inspire confidence in your decision making
- counter the tendency to rush to judgement.

The chart below gives a simple eight stage decision framework – nine if you include monitoring – that has been tested on several thousand managers, who reportedly found it helpful in making important choices.

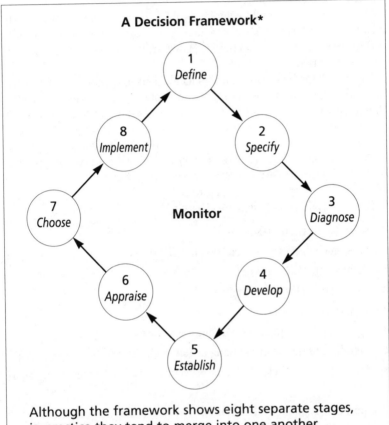

A Decision Framework*

1 Define

2 Specify

3 Diagnose

4 Develop

5 Establish

6 Appraise

7 Choose

8 Implement

Monitor

Although the framework shows eight separate stages, in practice they tend to merge into one another. Throughout the whole process you need to keep monitoring the situation and adjusting your approach.

While you would not use the framework to decide what TV programme to watch, it is a powerful tool for making sense of the decision process. It may take several tries to make it work, but you will soon find it gives your more important decision making a definite logical structure.

* Adapted from *How to Make a Business Decision*, by E. R. Archer, Management Review. February 1980, printed with permission of the publisher, copyright by A. Macom, a division of American Management Associations.

Decision analysis

Decision analysis is the formal title for a range of decision tools. These mainly quantify some aspect of the choice, throwing more light on the nature of the different outcomes.

Decision analysis solves complex problems by systematically evaluating alternatives. You can use it to make predictions and bring a more scientific approach to making choices. However, it complements rather than replaces intuition or judgement,

The best-known decision analysis tool is a sheet of paper divided down the middle, on which you record the pros and cons of different choices. Having listed all the arguments for and against a particular course of action, you review whether any pro cancels out a con. You thus eliminate items until you reach a few remaining factors that might determine the choice. This simple idea dates back to the eighteenth century and has since blossomed into some elaborate and often arcane statistical methods, some of which require specialist training to use.

Decision analysis brings more clarity to:

- who the decision makers are
- how much importance each person will have in making the final choice
- defining the alternatives
- solving complex problems
- making predictions
- specifying the criteria for judging the choices
- quantifying the risk of making different choices
- pinpointing obstacles likely to prevent desired outcomes from occurring.

Although decision analysis can improve the decision process, it is usually time consuming and costly. For instance, to analyse the environmental impact of a major investment decision, such as where to build an oil refinery, may take many months.

Decision analysis often relies on calculating the likelihood of an event occuring. For example, what is the chance of an earthquake happening in Tokyo as against one occurring in London? The resulting calculations are expressed in terms of probability, a term used to give risk a very precise meaning.

However, quantification often lends the whole procedure a spurious sense of scientific reliability. For example, assessing the chance of something happening as the result of a particular decision may rely almost entirely not on detailed statistics but on subjective estimates of the probabilities. On the other hand, decision analysis does make you define the problem more explicitly and demands a number of logical steps. It also forces you to document the whole process. However, the drawbacks are the time it takes and the way it adds extra complexity to the choice. It also requires that people co-operate in making it effective.

The tools

You do not need to learn all the many decision tools to be an effective manager. You do, however, need to be aware of what is available and be able to apply some of the simpler ones yourself.

Decision tools

- statistical methods: averages; dispersion; indices; time series; sampling; regression; probability distributions
- information systems: obtaining, analysing and evaluating relevant data
- decision models: methods to simulate the different decision situations
- linear programming: a statistical technique that takes into account the constraints in making important choices
- decision trees: a visual and numerical way of explaining choices and their various consequences.

While some of these tools are simple to use, even quite large companies often do not adopt them in the mistaken belief that they are too difficult or not appropriate. You do not need to be statistical genius to realise that some types of averages are more appropriate than others in certain situations. A grounding in basic statistics is certainly a minimum management competency these days.

Models We use mathematical models every day without even realising it. For example, calculating how long it will take to drive from one place to another requires an estimate of both distance and likely travelling speed to produce an expected arrival time. Models help replace rule of thumb decisions with a program that identifies the best or optimal decision.

Even without understanding the mathematics of a model, you cannot afford to be unaware of the assumptions underpinning it when they relate to your decisions. You may need to play a major part in determining which variables to include and which to ignore. You may even need to offer a subjective estimate of the probability of certain events occurring.

- Quantitative models involve rigorous logic and precision, usually at the expense of realism. They leave little room for any ambiguity since there are stated givens.

- Qualitative models are based on formulae which produce a simple, often elegant solution. Here the givens are less explicit.

You might expect to use such models for strategic, tactical and also operational purposes.

- Strategic models are used for: planning company objectives; planning policy; selecting locations for new factories; environmental impact planning; non-routine capital budgeting.

- Tactical models are used for: financial planning; manpower planning; designing plant layout; routine capital budgeting.

- Operational models are used for: credit ratings; media selection; production scheduling; inventory control; time and motion analysis; quality control.

New models are being produced all the time. These may simulate a market situation or solve a stock control problem. The mathematical techniques are also constantly being improved. There are some powerful low cost software packages that enable non-statisticians to do complex analysis without learning the actual mathematical techniques. For example, Crystal Ball for Windows (Decision Engineering, Denver) is a forecasting and risk management program that takes some of the mystery out of models. It helps answer such questions as: 'Will we stay under budget if we build this facility?'; 'What are the chances of this project finishing on time?'; or 'How likely are we to achieve this level of probability?' It uses a technique known as Monte Carlo simulation, although you never need to learn its mechanics. In essence it extends the forecasting capability of spreadsheets, which many managers use regularly for their decisions.

There are many other techniques, such as marginal analysis, utility theory and heuristics that also have highly specific uses in decision making. It would be useful to gain a general understanding of what these can do, without necessarily learning how to apply them in practice. The key to being an effective manager is understanding which tool to select, when to apply it and how to interpret the resulting information. In many cases it is best to seek expert help, although increasingly managers – and even those on the shop floor – are required to use the simpler tools such as basic statistical methods. These help unravel cause and effect and predict trends.

Group decision making

'How could I have been so stupid?' wailed President Kennedy after the fiasco of the abortive invasion of Cuba. Margaret Thatcher complained bitterly of being 'betrayed' by her cabinet colleagues, and in the London Stock Exchange the notorious Taurus computer system wasted millions of pounds and cost the Chief Executive his job. In all these examples, groups played an important role in what occurred.

Groups are an important part of most managers' decision making, whether or not they realise it. Because decision making is a process, groups can play a significant part at various stages, while not necessarily being directly involved in the actual final choice.

Groups or teams can improve your decision making because they can handle variety well and often save time in undertaking analysis. They can help reduce your own bias by bringing a wider perspective to the decision arena. They may help overcome resistance to getting a particular decision made or implemented. For example, the members will often have far more influence collectively than a single manager working unaided.

The danger of groups is that they sometimes reject diversity in the decision arena, and demand a damaging conformity. This is called *group think*, and happens when the members become over committed to a course of action and cease to be willing to look at the alternatives.

Group think occurs, for example, when a board of directors manages to convince itself, despite strong evidence to the contrary, that an investment is worthwhile. In the worst days of IBM's decline, for instance, group think appeared to take hold of the senior policy makers who seemed unable to accept overwhelming evidence that previous policies that had stood the company in good stead no longer worked. Much the same happened in General Motors, which took years to come to terms with the reality of Japanese quality.

Stress

Making choices is often highly stressful. When the corporate risks are high the possible consequences of a wrong judgement may be personally damaging. The stress occurs partly because one is entering unknown territory.

Too much stress obstructs decision making and leads to management by crisis. People no longer think coherently and fail to make choices at the right moment or make them irrationally. The most extreme example of this happening is panic, when our selection of alternatives is likely to be blind to even the most obvious consequences.

A common result of stress is decision paralysis. People delay or constantly postpone making a decision, while hunting for yet more information. A paralysis of analysis is a real danger. To counter this tendency, try to set firm deadlines by which a decision will be made. Sometimes any decision is better than no decision at all.

Many of the symptoms of stress are obvious, such as waking during the night, feeling anxious, lack of concentration, tiredness and so on. If you notice these signs take a break, have a long walk, do some exercise, meditate or do whatever relaxes you! Experienced managers who have just completed a long international air flight, for example, make no major decisions until they have unwound.

Creativity

Effective decision making requires creativity. We often tend to think of creativity as only being about inventing products or see it in the purely artistic sense. Sometimes it is seen as merely generating lists of ideas.

However, creativity contributes to all eight stages in the decision process described on page 73. Given that decision making is concerned with the future, we need to use many of the essentials of creativity to handle this forward thinking: curiosity, looking beyond the obvious, taking risks, wondering if there is a better way.

Creativity makes a special contribution when we must generate alternatives from which to choose. The more choices available, the better the chance of reaching a sound decision. Be creative in generating:

- different courses of action
- likely causes
- possible solutions
- a variety of outcomes.

Creativity is important because of the way it forces previously unacceptable courses of action to the surface. For example, the part-owner of Compaq computers wondered how the company could regain its previous market position. He had tried asking the Chief Executive to explain why the company was not doing well, but still felt dissatisfied with his answers. So he took a highly imaginative step.

He arranged for two independent engineers to buy on the open market all the components needed to build a Compaq computer. The result revealed that the company was paying too much for its components. By becoming more imaginative in its purchasing policy, it substantially reduced its overheads.

Ways of enhancing decision making through creativity

- *Brainstorming.* A large number of alternatives are generated by encouraging people to produce as many ideas as possible. All ideas are documented without initial criticism. Only after the idea-generating stage are they evaluated.

- *Free association.* The mind is allowed to roam over broad territory by linking one word, idea or a concept with another in a chain. It can be a highly focused activity or a general way of exploring alternatives.

- *Mind mapping.* This is a visual way of drawing links between disparate ideas in a non-linear way.

- *Checklists.* These ensure that we look at the problem or situation more systematically. They work best for straightforward situations.

- *Role playing.* Fresh insights are often gained into existing situations. It works well when trying to identify new alternatives, gain people's commitment to decisions and triggering new thinking about an old problem.

- *Drawing.* Drawing helps us get in touch with a part of our brain that may not usually have a chance to contribute to a decision.

- *Metaphors, analogies and images.* These can redefine the problem or decision. For example, seeing a company acquisition as a 'marriage', an 'act of war' or a soap opera' may provide powerful new insights into the choices.

Implementation

To implement a decision you may need to anticipate problems, gain other people's support for it, put a plan into effect and monitor it in action. Busy managers often rush into a decision without properly working out how they will implement it. For example, literally hundred of companies have plunged into total quality programmes based on a hasty decision with inadequate follow-through.

Having made a decision you ideally want to feel good about it. However, managers often suffer from *decisional regret*, and immediately begin undermining the implementation stage by attempting to reverse the decision in some way. For example, previously rejected alternatives are resurrected; originally unattractive choices now look more acceptable in the light of the decision that has just been made. Frequent changes of mind after a decision has been made suggest that some part of the decision process was not handled well. For example, insufficient alternatives may have been explored, or the criteria for judging them were not rigorous.

If this happens, act as if the choice cannot be reversed. This does not mean being blind to new information; it does mean having confidence in the choice that was originally made.

Contingencies

Contingency planning enables you to prepare for any unexpected consequences of your decision. They may be pleasant or unpleasant, and you should rank them according to:

● how *likely* the outcome is

● how *serious* it would be.

Next you start identifying preventive action to keep the decision on course. The more serious the outcome, the more you need to consider:

● how you would know the problem has arisen

● what actions might stop it happening

● whether you could eliminate the causes

● if you cannot eliminate the causes what might minimise their impact.

Commitment

A common complaint by managers is their difficulty in getting a decision implemented. This often reflects a failure to obtain commitment to the decision in the first place. You may need to work hard to gain people's support, and your success may depend on how you present your proposals, how enthusiastic you seem about them and whom you enrol in agreeing to proceed.

Most decisions go wrong, not from careless analysis, insufficient alternatives or poor information. The commonest reason is failing to gain enough support to see the decision through. When you think about decision making, two of your earliest concerns need to be:

● 'Whose help do I need to get to make it happen?'

● 'What do I need to do to gain their commitment?'

Further reading

LEIGH A. *Perfect Decisions*. London, Arrow Books, 1994

9 *nine*

Networking

Who would you call if you were fired? Who would you contact for hard to find information? Who do you know who knows someone who knows the person you need to know?

Networking is an essential life skill that no manager can do without these days. It has become more important as organisations and ways of working have changed. It is no longer enough to know who is directly above and below you, or even on a par with you. To be effective you need to be able to draw on contacts from a wide spectrum, across the entire organisation and beyond it. As organisations have de-layered, re-engineered, flattened and in many cases disintegrated into individual business units, getting things done is no longer just a case of issuing orders. To make things happen you have to know the right people.

Traditional organisations relied on self-contained units, a pyramid structure and communication channels, and a hierarchy of decision making. These worked for routine and stable enterprises and government agencies. In today's nimble-footed business environment, rapid change has increased the speed and quality of information needed on which to make decisions. Hence the need for more interpersonal contacts.

Seniority as a way of making important decisions may no longer work well. For example, it once required a senior manager to halt a car assembly production line. Today, in several firms, any production worker has the right to do so.

Another change has been the shift from negotiating with suppliers and customers, towards partnerships. Internal resources are used more flexibly and often within temporary project teams. With communication no longer just up and down, managers are part of a communications and information network.

Networking also needs to be seen in the wider context of the organisation's strategic intent. It is hard enough trying to design the future, but doing it alone is almost impossible. Networking is an important way of gaining a collective view of what the future might look like, and drawing on resources for implementing change.

The management role

What separates successful from unsuccessful managers, particularly at senior level, is their networking abilities. Most managers now spend their time in lateral rather than vertical relationships, and that is happening at an increasing rate in many fast moving organisations. Interpersonal skills are therefore important, and networking demands that these skills should be of a high order.

Effective managers work at building contacts in other departments so that, when required, they can obtain rapid co-operation. They know that seniority alone will not guarantee such help. It will take the construction of personal relationships.

Networks are loosely constructed arrangements that bypass the hierarchy. Whoever initiates a project, for instance, will be responsible for seeing it through, regardless of their position in the organisation. If you work in an organisation that relies heavily on projects or temporary teams, you will need an anchor as you move from one group to another. A network provides that support.

Networks facilitate direct person-to-person connections. This might be through phone calls, meetings, faxes, video conferences, E-mail and so on. Instead of having around you one specific team, as a manager expert at networking you also have a 'virtual' team you can call on at any time.

Learning the art of networking is becoming critical to managerial success. It matters most in organisations that are:

- strongly decentralised
- based on heavy interdependence between people of different knowledge and skills
- based on common and demanding standards of performance
- willing to allow leadership to be exercised by informal leaders
- ready to accept challenges to traditional boundaries.

In these organisations, networkers may be unacquainted with each other yet willing to help when contacted. There may be few fixed relationships and many diverse skills. Those who are appointed to run various kinds of teams may not be the most senior people, but are able to call on important resources. There is therefore a high degree of sharing and trust amongst network members. Different opinions are valued and there is considerable openness and information sharing.

Benefits of Networking

To you:

- more contacts leading to more business
- the wider knowledge and service you can offer others
- more exposure and a higher profile
- opportunities to learn
- improved cover for periods of illness
- formal and informal support for projects/problems
- a variety of information
- the chance to offload worries and be listened to
- career enhancement
- constructive feedback
- celebration of success
- help in confronting senior people
- assistance in deciding priorities.

To others:

- better service
- more business
- the chance to share your knowledge and expertise
- promotion of the organisation
- speedy problem solving.

Anyone can form a network. All it needs is people who are flexible, willing to take responsibility and understand how their work dovetails into other people's.

You may never know the full benefits of your network since it can help you without you even realising if. People come your way, contacts emerge, knowledge somehow arrives, things happen. Good networkers trust that it will work for them, and they put in as much as they take out.

The network is everywhere

An executive making a career change on his return from a long overseas assignment reported an exciting week because he had been to two funerals. 'You won't believe the people I met there,' he told a colleague. 'I met two head hunters, a company director and one of my cousins who is personal assistant to the chief executive of a major company.'

This manager knew few people in town and embarked on a determined networking effort. He organised a party of old school friends, many of whom had become successful since leaving school. He kept scrupulous notes of meetings, contacts and other interactions. He was polite and courteous to people who spent time with him. He maintained the contacts he had made, and eventually he was offered a job.

You never know when the network will come in handy. So keep up the contacts, for months, even years, and eventually it will pay off. The connections may be so extraordinary that looking back on them it scarcely seems credible that such tenuous links led to a solution. But dedicated networkers know that the links are never entirely clear or predictable; they just trust that they will somehow deliver. In my own company, for example, we regularly 'put out a call' to the network, asking for help. Does anyone know a brilliant administrator, has anyone heard of an inexpensive odd job person, has anyone a contact into a particular company? Each time we are surprised at the convoluted route the answer has taken to reach us.

Over 300 professional women in Britain and the USA were asked by Sundridge Park Management Centre why they joined or did not join networks and what they got out of them.

British women found networks valuable for the social contacts they gave, whereas the American women had a much more focused approach and viewed them as business arenas. While British women saw networks as ways to meet people with similar interests their US counterparts tended to leave a network if it did not lead to business and job opportunities.

Amongst women there is often the feeling that networking is something only men do in their golf clubs and through the 'old school tie'. This reluctance is rapidly disappearing. There are now scores of women's networks, including City Women's Network, Forum, Focus and Women in Business. There is even one that creates a web of contacts amongst women who attended certain private schools.

Networks enable organisations to compete in a highly volatile climate. No traditional corporate structure, regardless of how de-layered and uncluttered it becomes, can match the speed, flexibility and focus that business success demands. Networks are fast, smart and fluid. They can reshape how business decisions are made. In effect a network can identify the small company inside the large company. It enables the right people to converge faster, in a more focused way.

Building your network

It is said that if you want a parcel delivered by hand to someone in Saskatchewan you only need start with seven people in the room. Those seven will know other people who know other people, who will eventually identify someone who just happens to be going to Saskatchewan.

In the best network relationships you do someone a favour, asking nothing in return. Some time later, maybe weeks, months or even years, you receive a favour back from someone else in the network. Nobody keeps a score – the network works because people want it to.

The focus of networks is on getting things done rather than on procedures. They are a way of making things happen that often bypass traditional systems and structures that might otherwise get in the way or slow things down. One of the unwritten principles of successful networking is the *Law of Hidden Returns*. This law says that whatever you put into a network will eventually come back to you, perhaps multiplied several times over. You may never really know how, when or even why this happens. Often the return is invisible, yet it happens. You just assume that the system works in your favour – you trust that it does. There is nothing mystical or metaphysical about the Law of Hidden Returns. You merely rely on the fact that what makes networks succeed is that, like teamwork, the sum is greater than the parts.

Making contacts for your network can be a passive or an active process. Passive contact building is slow, occurring naturally as you do your daily work. You extend the web by raising your awareness of how people might fit into your network and discussing with them ways of co-operating. The more you know about the people you meet the better placed you are to see whether or how they can fit into your network. What are their skills and experience, who do they know, what are their goals and how might you help them achieve them?

People network by joining clubs, going to lunch with friends, attending conferences, joining industry associations, going to reunion dinners and staying in touch. They network with church members, school friends and community organisations.

The key to networking is spending significant time developing new contacts and managing the old ones. People need calling, meeting, lunching, contacting. A network is more than just a list of people or a little black book, although you can make notes of the people in it. You cannot make networking succeed for you by treating it like a bumper-car ride – arriving two minutes before a meeting starts, never making a contribution, making little or no time to get to know people.

Active contact building means building lists, and constantly refining them. It includes everything from Christmas cards to phone calls, from lunches to sending someone the odd article about some topic you know they are interested in. You should look for excuses to call, to write, to meet. It can be time consuming and, if you pick the wrong people, incredibly wasteful. But with the right people, your efforts will be amply justified.

Some Networking Basics

Be cautious at the start. Make the first move and avoid making it a request. Sending out your promotional literature is not networking, it is selling.

Be prepared. Help other people. List the members of your network on index cards or a computer. Note down information that may be of use to them when you hear it.

Find the right approach. You have to decide which member to approach with your request and how to make it. When making a request do not always seek the obvious; try to get different answers or perspectives on an issue.

Avoid pressure. People like to be approached gradually, not hustled into helping you. Carefully assess the ability of the person you plan to ask.

Use people's time wisely. Know what you want before you ask for it. Think things through before picking up the phone.

Check for reasonableness. Consider whether your request is reasonable. Are you asking someone to take a big risk? Will it require much time and money? If the tables were turned would you do it for the other person?

Respect their priorities. Even though your request is important to you, the other person may be too busy right now to help. Accept this with good grace.

Be specific. If you are vague you may not get what you want. Calling half a dozen people may be useless if they are the wrong ones. Explain what you need and why. Ask them how they would approach the same problem.

Think about the phrasing. Give thought to how you convey your requests. Phrasing requests like sales patter may be less effective than if offered as opportunities or possibilities.

Reciprocate. If someone asks you for help, give it generously. If you cannot provide it, recommend someone else to contact. Show a real interest in their problem.

Give value. Offer value rather than always trying to make a sale. If you always speak at conferences, write articles, or join associations just to make a sale you will turn people off. Give value without expecting anything in return.

More Network Principles

Keep people informed. When given the name of someone to call, keep your original contact informed about any results.

Use people's names with respect. People letting you use their names assume that you will offer others the same service you gave them.

Say thank you. Never take someone's good nature for granted; a thank you is always required.

Start now. Do not wait until you really need a network to begin developing one. Networks are based on trust, respect and personal chemistry. They are not created overnight.

Stay in touch. Networks continually change, evolve, expand and contract. They need nurturing; be creative about keeping in touch.

Keep it two way. Maintain a balance between asking for and giving help. Too much giving is as bad as too much taking. By giving without ever accepting something in return, you make recipients hesitant to ask for more; you imply that they have nothing to offer.

Deliver on promises. Do not make promises you cannot deliver.

Spread the load. Avoid over-reliance on one person; this can destroy the best of relationships.

Be human. If someone asks for your help about a problem they have been wrestling with for weeks, the last thing they want is for you to solve it in seconds. This implies that they have overlooked the obvious and are stupid. Try asking questions that lead them to a solution by themselves.

Treat in confidence. Do not share sensitive or confidential information with anyone else. If your sources realise you are unreliable, they will cease trusting you.

Don't judge. Avoid passing judgements on someone's request for help. Even if it seems foolish to you, they may have important reasons they cannot reveal.

When you create a formal network such as an interest group that meets regularly to share information or explore common problems, you may need some written documentation to clarify what people should expect. Someone may need to take responsibility for running the network, for example, by sending out information or calling meetings.

Draw your network

What does your network of relationships look like? Try drawing it out and you will probably find it is larger than you think. Use a large A3 sheet of paper to develop a framework like the one on page 89. It is usually easier to start with internal relationships. Identify who is above you in the vertical chain. Only show people on your network where you have a direct one-to-one relationship with them. If you never speak to the boss's boss, that person is not really on your network.

If you work in a large organisation, you might also trying dividing the relationships into divisions, groups and so on. Also, avoid listing people who just happen to have the same job title. You are trying to chart genuine connections, not formal organisational arrangements.

Network meetings

While some networks are 'virtual' ones, that is the people in them seldom or never actually meet, many are maintained by regular meetings. The smooth running of a network depends on the effectiveness of these meetings and it can be sensible to have one person chairing it and another managing the time keeping.

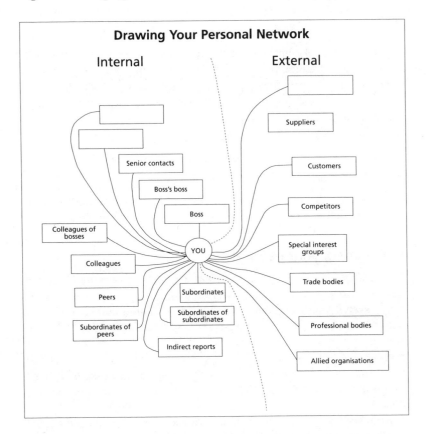

The meetings might be of several kinds, for example educational, networking and training events. The educational meetings might involve outside speakers and group members contributing their experience. Networking meetings would have as their main aim the achievement of every member's individual goals.

Analysing network relationships

● What do they want from me?
● What do I want from them?
● How do they tell me what they want?

- How do I tell them what I want?

- What are the main issues or things involved in the exchanges I have with them?

- How do I know if my or their performance is satisfactory?

- How do the relationships vary in type, importance, degree of interdependence, strength, political closeness, nurturing, intensity, formality, effectiveness. Are they upwards or downwards in the hierarchy, giving or taking, static or dynamic, comfortable or difficult, social or business?

- What can I do to strengthen the relationship?

- Is enough time being invested in a particular relationship?

- Is the networking helping me to be more effective?

- How could the network serve me better and what action must I take to ensure that it does?

Maintaining your network

Networking managers soon realise that they must give as much as they get. Doing someone on your network a favour can be immensely satisfying, even if you never talk to them directly about it. For example, you may get a call for help from a person who has been recommended to call you by one of your network contacts. You owe this unknown person nothing and may never see or speak to them again. Yet because they have come through the network you should spend real time with them. When they say how helpful it has been, you have done your network duty.

Keep seeking ways to build your network, even if you keep it a small one. The quality of the contacts is often more important than the quantity. Also, try discussing your network with your boss. He or she may have their own contribution to make in building yours.

Networks have a life of their own and need handling like any other change process. Moving into a new managerial position, effective managers spend a considerable time building their network of co-operative relationships. They work hard at building links with those they believe will help them make a successful impact in the new role.

No matter how much power you acquire you cannot escape the fact that your job involves political awareness. You need to understand the various political factions, formal and personal alliances and the leaders who may help you succeed in your job. For example, do you have your superior's secretary on your network? This can be a key relationship for gaining inside information and seeding ideas.

Look for gaps in your network and try to plug them. Similarly, be willing to weaken or sever relationships that have no hope of being productive in the long term. It is no use cluttering your contact list with hundreds of names if you either cannot devote time to them or if they are unlikely to be of practical use. In building and maintaining your network you will always be:

- initiating contacts
- testing and reviewing relationships
- developing key contacts.

The blocks

Some managers remain reluctant networkers. They find the whole process distasteful or messy. Often this reluctance reflects a defensiveness that ultimately damages their effectiveness. Shyness is another reason for avoiding active networking. It takes a certain amount of confidence to call someone you do not know and ask for help. But one of the commonest reasons why people fail to make networking succeed is that they simply forget people's names, lose their phone numbers, or fail to keep proper records.

If you are reluctant to network it is time to explore the barriers and see if you can begin to overcome them. If you are shy, then maybe you could benefit from some personal development programme to build your confidence. If you keep losing names, use a computer based contact system, or more simply use a business card holder book. If you are unsure who might be useful as a network contact, try discussing with people how you might co-operate.

Although networks are powerful ways of getting practical help, they are not meant to be therapy groups. Although networking may be therapeutic, it is not usually meant for that purpose. The exhilaration of talking to others who are active, concerned listeners should not be allowed to crowd out other activities and aims.

Nor should the situation be allowed to become highly competitive. If you vie for leadership and group control you will not be helping the network, especially if this is done in a win/lose way.

Networks are a recipe for personal and organisational success. Nurture yours and it will repay you many times over.

Further reading

SMITH B. 'Networking for real'. *Journal of European Industrial Training.* Vol. 13, No. 4, 1989

SONNENBERG F. 'The professional (and personal) profits of networking.' *Training and Development Journal.* September 1990

10 *ten*

Force Field Analysis

How many people must you convince in order to make something happen in an organisation – 10, 30, 75 per cent, everyone? How many do you need to support you in achieving even a simple change?

Critical mass is one of the secrets of making things happen in organisations. You do not need to get everyone on your side, or even half or a quarter of the people around you. You only need a sufficient number of people to support you, or at least not to try to stop you, so that your desired change gains an almost irresistible momentum. You need far fewer people than you probably think to obtain critical mass.

Critical mass arises when there are enough people beginning to make it hard to say no to what you want to do. This could be as few as two people, or it could be a dozen. It is seldom more than a handful. However, you need to identify them carefully since they are the people with power – power to say no, to say yes or to block progress. Some may be relatively low in the formal pecking order, yet have considerable influence.

You can achieve extraordinary changes with critical mass. In essence it is a kind of lever, a way of creating change using a minimum amount of force. The principle behind it is the use of leverage. This is also at the root of the widely used business skill called *force field analysis* (FFA), which can be used in conjunction with critical mass.

FFA has been around a considerable time, and it has outlasted many management panaceas that have since vanished into obscurity. It has survived because several generations of practising managers have found that it works, and helps them do their job more effectively.

The assumption of FFA

A basic assumption of FFA is:

93

● At a given moment, any situation in an organisation is in a brief state of equilibrium.

If you have learned science at school or college you will probably recognise this assumption as being similar to Newton's law that a body will be at rest when all the forces acting on it cancel each other out.

Unfortunately it is not quite that simple. Organisations are more likely to conform, not to Newton's idea of physics, but those of quantum mechanics. In the latter nothing is ever in equilibrium. You cannot even be sure you can describe how things are, since to know one thing for certain means remaining unsure of another. Organisations are complex systems. Assuming that they are stable is comforting but wrong. They are in a continuous state of change, although this may not be immediately obvious.

Any equilibrium is not only short lived, it is often illusory. There is no indefinite *status quo*, only a dynamic tension between the various counteracting forces on any temporary *status quo*. Acting on the equilbrium are:

● restraining forces
● driving forces.

The chart on page 95 shows the equilibrium situation in an organisation and also a change that someone would like to make. In essence the two sets of forces are the natural checks and balances that make up not only organisations, but also the universe. When you disturb the checks and alter the balance, something new begins to happen.

As I have said, no organisation is ever entirely in equilibrium. It is constantly in a state of flux and it would be unwise to assume that any *status quo* will last long. Yet FFA works just as well even in a fast changing environment, so long as you use it strictly as a way of looking analytically at how to achieve change.

FFA in action

Suppose some people in an organisation decide that it is time to launch a new product. They may have well developed ideas about this product, and how much it should cost and who will buy it. Supporting their argument are some important driving forces:

● The company badly needs a new product range.
● Profit margins of existing lines have fallen sharply.
● The company has a good reserve of cash.
● A new marketing director has recently arrived and is talking about identifying profitable new opportunities.

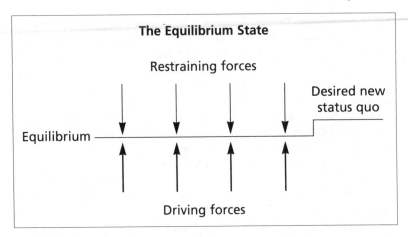

The Equilibrium State

Restraining forces

Desired new
status quo

Equilibrium

Driving forces

However, the natural checks and balances in the organisation mean that although the proposers of the new product have some allies, there are problems:

- There are people who are not yet convinced.
- Others disagree that the time is right for such expenditure.
- There are also important factors militating against a new product launch.
- The actual cost of development will be high.
- The product development manager is retiring shortly and is anxious not to leave on a failure.
- The sales force has no experience of the new product area.

Right now these factors just about cancel each other out. There is an impasse, even though many people see the urgency of launching a new product line. So nothing much is changing. In effect, the company is stuck with the *status quo*.

What can the new product developers do? They need to create sufficient critical mass to make it is impossible to obstruct the work of developing a new product. Yet how do they do that? Using FFA language, they can either:

- strengthen the driving forces for change
- weaken the restraining forces for change.

The driving forces, which include the need for a new product range, reduced profit margins, cash reserves and a new marketing director, are all pushing towards upsetting the equilibrium. The restraining forces, which include high development costs, the product development manager and the inexperience of the sales force, are tending to act against any change.

In critical mass, you do not need to convince everyone to go along with what you want. Likewise with FFA you do not need to alter all the driving and restraining forces. Just changing one or two may be enough to break the impasse and precipitate change.

In our new product example, the enthusiasts for the new venture might strengthen the driving forces by forming a new product committee chaired by the new marketing director. This might increase his commitment and be enough to get things moving. Or they might try to weaken the restraining forces by gaining the support of the head of personnel, who could encourage the existing product development manager to take early retirement.

Once the equilibrium of driving and restraining forces is disturbed the change can begin. But the situation may not necessarily turn out as expected. Organisations consist of people, and we cannot easily predict precisely how everyone will respond. Altering the driving or restraining forces may produce unexpected outcomes.

Altering the driving and restraining forces that currently maintain a particular situation therefore has its risks. It could lead to the achievement of the new goal and creation of a new equilibrium. On the other hand it might result in:

- a return to the previous equilibrium
- the eventual establishment of a new, unexpected equilibrium
- long term destabilisation.

The first result might occur if the new product enthusiasts got their way, and a new sales line was launched in a test market, but did not immediately achieve outstanding success. There could then be a loss of confidence and insufficient investment, leading to the new line being withdrawn after a year and the company returning broadly to the way it was previously. This actually happened to the Disney Corporation shortly after its founder died. Nothing seemed to offer the same spectacular returns as Mickey Mouse. So the company kept killing off new ideas, and entering new markets half-heartedly or not at all.

A dramatic example of the second result was when Ford motors invented the E-coat method of improving the quality of paintwork, particularly the rust-proofing of the undersides of vehicles. This ingenious process used an electrical charge to attract paint to all the hard-to-reach nooks and crannies of a vehicle and was a stunning success.

Ford was first with E-coat and it became the industry standard. General Motors adopted it and paid Ford a royalty, as did the Japanese. Yet a major restraining force was the cost of converting all Ford's factories. By the time it did, competition from the Japanese was acute, one of their assets being excellent paint work. Virtually all major car manufacturers had the system and a new equilibrium was established in this area, but not one Ford ever expected or desired.

Using FFA

FFA focuses attention on the power of driving and restraining forces. Using it involves a mixture of defining the problem or situation, then reviewing the various forces to see how best to affect them.

Step 1   State the problem area

What do you want to achieve or change? First state the situation as you see it, by defining the broad topic area. You might be concerned for instance about an issue to do with personnel, marketing, production or administration. The problem must be a real one and sufficiently important to be worth trying to resolve. State the exact problem area that represents the present equilibrium, for example:

● sales of a particular product

● personal remuneration

● rejects in manufacturing

● the quality of our service.

These problem definitions state the boundaries of the situation which you want to alter.

Step 2   Define the situation

Next describe the situation in terms of the status quo you want to affect. For example:

● We need to sell much more product.

● I should receive a big pay increase.

● We must have far fewer rejects in our manufacturing.

● The quality of our service needs to improve radically.

Try to state the exact nature of the change you want, expressed for instance in how much more product should be sold, how large a pay rise you want and so on.

A problem defined is often a problem half solved. So it pays to spend time producing a tight specification of the shift in the status quo you want. If you are going to attempt to upset the equilibrium it makes sense to know what you are trying to achieve.

Step 3   Specify the new equilibrium

Nail down a tight description of the new equilibrium. This is a goal statement of how the situation will look once the restraining or driving forces have been altered and new ones have come into operation.

Express the goal in quantified form, or at least provide some measurable way of deciding whether the new equilibrium has actually been reached. For example:

● Sales of product are at a new norm of 20,000 a month.

● My new salary is 30 per cent more than my present one.

● We have a maximum reject rate of one part per million.

● Our services are the most comprehensive in the industry.

Step 4   Analyse the forces

Now create two separate lists identifying what you see as the restraining and driving forces. These lists may emerge from a brainstorming session or detailed organisational research. You need to know the forces currently at work, not those that might arise in the future or have recently ceased to exist. You might also choose to classify these two sorts of forces further into whether they are strong, medium or weak. This helps to decide where you are going to apply leverage to alter one of them. You could use a chart similar to the one on page 99.

A complicated force may need to be broken down further to make it easier to decide what might be done about it. For example, suppose that one of the restraining forces is identified as:

● The sales force has no experience of the new product area.

This might be further broken down into:

● The sales director is worried that he will be blamed for any failure of a new product.
● The cost of retraining the sales force is high.
● The new product line requires the sales force to operate portable computers linked to head office by modems; many sales staff will find it hard to adjust to the new technology.

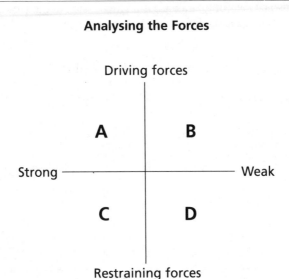

Analysing the Forces

Driving forces

A   B

Strong ——————————|—————————— Weak

C   D

Restraining forces

Having analysed the forces into these four segments, you may conclude that it is better to affect those falling into segment A rather than those in segment B.

Similarly, after further analysis, you may conclude that the restraining forces in the C segment are too hard to influence and it is better to spend time trying to further weaken the restraining forces in segment D.

It may also be worth dividing these into:

- *personal forces* – ones that deal with attitudes, feelings, weaknesses, relationships, education, income etc.
- *relationship forces* – ones that deal with how different individuals and groups relate to one another, such as the organisation and government, the department and a customer, the team and other teams, etc.
- *systems forces* – ones that form the organisation's environment, including political, social, legal, environmental and local conditions.

Categorising forces this way is helpful if it gives an added perspective to what you might do about them. Otherwise the headings are just another form of label.

It can also be helpful to draw a visual impression of the various forces for and against the change you want to make, as shown in the chart below.

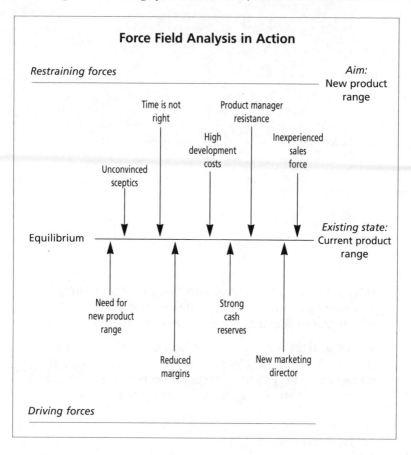

Force Field Analysis in Action

Restraining forces

Aim:
New product range

Time is not right

Product manager resistance

High development costs

Inexperienced sales force

Unconvinced sceptics

Equilibrium

Existing state:
Current product range

Need for new product range

Strong cash reserves

Reduced margins

New marketing director

Driving forces

Step 5   Devise a strategy

Having identified and perhaps visually portrayed the various driving and restraining forces, you need a strategy for altering the status quo. You will rarely possess enough time or knowledge to influence all the forces. As we saw on page 93, this is not necessary anyway. With the situation in temporary equilibrium all you need to do is locate one force susceptible to your influence.

Selecting a force to alter is like an army commander probing for the enemy's weak spot. It is seldom necessary to find more than one; the trick is to exploit it to the full. In reality, of course, you may not know precisely how strong the various forces are and what impact changing them will have. It is generally better to strengthen those driving forces that do not increase resistance to change, or to work on weakening restraining forces that do not precipitate an excessive reaction with highly unpredictable consequences.

In the example described on pages 94–97, one possibility would be to try to influence the early retirement of the product development manager. Such action would be highly political and might unleash all kinds of consequences. If the product manager is a powerful figure he might resent such an attempt and retaliate against whoever tried to engineer it.

If you are unsure about the relative importance of the various forces, the best strategy may be a mixture of weakening a restraining force and strengthening a driving force.

Step 6   Develop an action plan

Once you have decided on a strategy for affecting one or more of the forces, you need a detailed plan of action. This should consist of some highly practical tasks where there is clarity about what is to be attempted and by whom.

Keep the various steps of your action plan simple. Affecting the equilibrium may take several actions. Go for small successes rather than one large one. To have a real effect on a driving force you will need to be determined and able to decide whether or not your strategy is working.

Step 7   Establish a new equilibrium

Once you have set change in motion there is a danger of it getting out of control. Revolutionaries are often consumed by their own creation and if you are not careful this may happen to you too. For example, suppose in their enthusiasm for weakening one of the restraining forces the new product enthusiasts persuaded the head of personnel to consider the early retirement option. This might lead to a decision to introduce some compulsory redundancies.

Once an equilibrium has been disturbed, there is always the chance that the original goal will be reached and then left behind. A new, undesirable situation may be created instead. A typical example of this is when a company makes a takeover bid for another company and, having succeeded, finds that it has attracted the unwelcome attentions of a predator.

Most organisations also have a natural inertia. Even if the equilibrium is successfully altered and a new situation created, there is always the risk of a gradual return to the previous status quo. To institutionalise change the new equilibrium must become essential to the organisation. For example, there must be powerful restraining forces preventing any return to the previous position.

FFA offers a simple framework to help you decide what action to take. It reduces problems to a manageable size and stimulates new courses of action. When situations look set in concrete, FFA can often reveal that a careful alteration of the driving and restraining forces is not only possible but relatively easy.

It tends to encourage an optimistic view about making things happen and is attractive because it can be used by a single person or a large group. Using FFA with your own team, you will also discover that it promotes a common understanding of a situation and encourages better team work. Once people have worked their way through the analysis they are also usually more committed to affecting the change. It depends for its success on the quality and completeness of the analytical work, however. If you do not properly identify the main driving or restraining forces you may choose one that is too weak to make much difference.

Further reading

LEIGH A. *Effective Change.* (Chapter Fifteen.) London, IPM, 1988

11 *eleven*

Problem People

Problem people are the ones you complain about. They are the ones you have tried to persuade to do what you want, but still cause difficulties. They require more of your time than anyone else, causing you headaches in countless ways. Yet these same people often have marvellous ideas, generate change without realising it, and have something valuable to offer.

So what do we really mean by a problem person? It is normally someone who does poor work, is a bad time keeper, resists change, constantly upsets other people, fails to speak enough, misses deadlines, annoys clients, and so on.

Even experienced managers will sometimes say, 'I've run out of ideas on how to deal with him' or 'She could do so much better, but I just can't seem to make any progress' or 'He simply never does what I ask.' These are all signs that there is a problem person to be managed.

Since problem people can be incredibly effective under different circumstances, it is better to think of them as a symptom as much as a problem. It is their behaviour you need to alter, not their personality.

In the wider context of the organisation's future strategic intentions, your identification and handling of so-called problem people may prove extremely important. Often problem people are the ones who are pressing for the organisation to do things differently, challenging the status quo and seeing the world as it really is, not as it is defined by long serving managers.

Being a better manager can therefore mean challenging people's perceptions of who is seen as a problem person and why. You can for example, question whether the future of the company is really being undermined by these people, or whether in fact they are serving it. All organisations, for instance, need mavericks. As Anita Roddick of The Body Shop has argued, if you find the mavericks you will find those who can help you define the future.

There are many ways of dealing with problem behaviour, including:

- coaching (see Chapter 4)
- counselling
- appraisal interviews (see Chapter 3)
- training
- confrontation
- job restructuring
- neutralising
- transferring
- punishment
- dismissal.

Some informal ways of tackling problem behaviour

- Ignore it.
- Delay your reaction and play for time.
- Allow yourself to be overwhelmed by it.
- Stand firm and decare your boundaries and limits.
- Yield and accept it.
- Acknowledge and tolerate it and then move on.
- Change or adapt your own behaviour.
- Try to influence the other person to change.
- Pull rank and get the system to exert pressure.
- Define the situation as a shared problem and seek a contract to resolve it.
- Seek help in relating to the difficult person.

Defining problem behaviour

When asked to describe some of their problem employees managers often use words and phrases like 'lazy', 'poorly motivated', 'negative', 'devious', 'vague', 'living' in a world of their own', and so on. These descriptions all assume that they know what is going on in the other person's mind. To manage someone's adverse behaviour you need to become more specific. For example, does 'lazy', mean that the person arrives late every morning, or only on Tuesdays and Fridays? Can you explain with examples what you mean by being negative? Do they make disparaging remarks about other employees, about the company, about themselves?

Tackling adverse behaviour means giving less attention to feelings or intangible motivations. Instead you should focus on obsei consequences, and ask yourself whether you could measure the extent ʊ. this undesired behaviour if you wanted to. Saying that someone is lazy does not help you to manage them. Saying that they are always late is not much better if they generally arrive on time. If you can measure or at least define the adverse behaviour, with practical examples, you stand a better chance of being able to decide what to do about it.

You should also ask whether you actually need to alter the person's behaviour. Is it really so troublesome that a change is essential? Tolerating individual differences is an essential requirement in successful organisations and helps make an effective team.

What could be triggering the adverse behaviour? This does not require you to be clairvoyant, merely willing to investigate the behaviour and what might be causing it.

Internal Factors	External Factors
Has poor motivation	Meets boyfriend who finishes early
Dislikes meetings	Meetings last too long
Is a poor time keeper	Has a faulty watch
Has low morale	Is exhausted from overwork
Is bored	Has just been paid
Has a low drive	Contributions usually ignored
Lacks ideas	Is seldom asked for an opinion
Is impatient	Has an excessive workload
Has poor concentration	Is unwell

Causes may therefore be from outside sources and some of these may be within your own control. For example, a lack of job knowledge, group pressures, poor induction, ineffective training, weak quality procedures, working conditions and cultural differences may all be ones that you can tackle.

If you can uncover such causes you are halfway to finding an appropriate solution. Sadly though, it is never quite as easy as that, so you may decide instead to resort to behaviour modification, which is less concerned with causes and more with outcomes.

Modifying behaviours

The three simple rules of change are:

- It is easier to change the situation than the behaviour.
- It is easier to change the behaviour than the attitude.
- It is easier to change the attitude than the person.

Behaviour modification (BM) has nothing to do with brainwashing or other dubious procedures. It is merely applying some basic rules to affect other people's behaviour. These come from a mixture of psychological research and practical experience. Nor do you need to be psychologist to use them.

The essence of BM is that you ignore the many possible causes behind someone's behaviour. Instead of exploring motivations, feelings or even attitudes, you focus on actions.

As a practising manager you are affecting people's performance all the time, though without necessarily giving it a fancy name like behaviour modification. For example, you issue new work schedules, ask people to write reports, request them to undertake projects, meet customers, and so on. The question is not *whether* you will influence behaviour, but *how*.

BM assumes that you influence a person's behaviour by:

- affecting the triggers or cues that precede someone's behaviour
- rewarding the results of behaviour.

We touched on the first of these when we explored the possible causes of adverse behaviour. A trigger is any event which produces the behaviour you are concerned about. You may alter it, eliminate it or use awareness of the trigger to help the person change their response. For example, if every time you tell someone to be sure their report is on time it arrives late, then perhaps the person is responding to a trigger. It could be anything from a deep seated resentment about not being trusted to a dislike of having deadlines imposed without discussion.

With BM you do not necessarily seek to unravel the factors behind the trigger. You merely alter or remove the trigger. You concentrate on external events only, not the ones that may be going on inside someone's head. So, for instance, instead of always saying, 'Make sure this report is on time', you might change your approach and ask the person when they think they can deliver it.

The second of the two ways of affecting someone's behaviour is the result of behaviour itself. BM assumes that people learn the consequences of their behaviour.

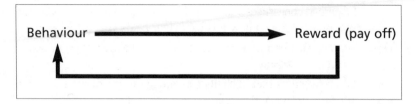

Suppose that each time your sales force reaches its monthly target you raise it for the following month. The sales force is likely to conclude that the penalty of success will be an even tougher job the next month. Adverse behaviour is therefore learned as a direct result of its consequences.

In essence, people conclude that there is a reward or pay off for acting in a certain way. In our sales example the reward for hitting a monthly target is a form of punishment. Discover what reward or pay off a person receives for the behaviour and you unlock the key to influencing them.

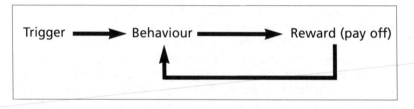

Another important aspect of using BM is the dual nature of rewards. People's behaviour can be influenced by rewards in two distinct ways. It can be:

- strengthened (reinforced)
- weakened (discouraged).

In strengthening someone's behaviour you positively reward them for doing something you want. For instance, if you smile every time one of your direct reports says 'Good morning' to you, you are positively rewarding their behaviour.

Altering behaviour through reinforcement

Step 1 Decide what you want the new behaviour to be.

Step 2 Identify the stages needed to get there.

Step 3 Watch for any sign of behaviour moving towards the first stage.

Step 4 At the first sign of behaviour in the desired direction, describe to the person concerned what they did, and offer encouragement and recognition. Explain how this behaviour helps you or the team.

Step 5 Continue reinforcing whenever the desired behaviour occurs, until it seems permanent.

Step 6 Watch for signs that behaviour is moving in the desired direction of the next stage and reinforce.

Similarly in weakening someone's behaviour your 'reward' takes the form of a negative response, that is punishment. For instance, if every time someone who reports to you arrives late at a meeting you scowl at them, you are sending a message that you disapprove of their behaviour.

The trouble with punishment is that it is easily misunderstood. For example, if you tend to frown in concentration each time someone makes a suggestion, they may see this as discouragement. By weakening their behaviour of making suggestions you could be starting to reward them for not making suggestions – that is, you will not frown if they stop making suggestions. You will often discover when using BM that you are inadvertently either rewarding undesirable behaviour, and thus encouraging it, or mistakenly punishing good behaviour.

Suppose someone keeps phoning you for approval every time they want to make even a minor decision. The constant calls interrupt your work and yet you always listen sympathetically, offer advice and ask pertinent questions until the person rings off. By asking, 'What is my subordinate's reward (pay off) for calling me?' you may begin to identify how to change the person's actions. For instance you may identify the rewards of calling you up constantly as:

- gains detailed advice
- shares the decision load
- avoids making a decision unaided
- feels important in being able to interrupt the boss.

If you conclude that the reward for ringing you is that the person does not shoulder responsibility, you should now reverse your approach. Next time the person rings asking for help with a minor decision you might withhold the reward. Instead of offering advice and prolonged listening, you might listen in a totally non-committal way and indicate you have limited time available. Soon the employee learns that calls about minor decisions do not gain the desired response. If you also congratulated the person for making minor decisions without calling you up first, this would reinforce their behaviour. They would tend to want to do more of it.

The 12 dos of behaviour modification:

- Choose an appropriate reward or punishment.
- Supply ample feedback.
- Recognise that different people need different rewards.
- Reinforce constructive behaviour.
- Schedule rewards intermittently.
- Ensure that rewards/punishments quickly follow observed behaviour.
- Remember that ignoring certain sorts of behaviour may eliminate it.
- Tell people what they must do to be rewarded.
- Punish people in private, not in front of others.
- Make rewards or punishments fit the behaviour.
- Change the rewards periodically.
- Reward only real changes in behaviour.

So the essence of behaviour modification is:

- Catch people doing something right and encourage them to do more of it.

Confrontation

Fear often makes us reject confrontation because we wish to avoid an unpleasant scene, perhaps because of our inability to handle our own emotions. Yet confrontation need not be a miserable experience. It can even be satisfying and inspiring.

Direct confrontation means tackling adverse behaviour as it occurs, or shortly afterwards. For example, in our own team the rule is to confront someone within two weeks if they behave unacceptably. Otherwise the issue is considered dead. This prevents resentment smouldering and gnawing away at our mutual respect and trust.

Confront by telling the truth, in a kind or loving way. This either gets what you want, or helps the other person learn and grow. Effective confrontation starts with an 'I' statement, about what you want. Avoid indirect statements such as 'The team feels . . .', 'The company would like . . .', or 'One just does not do that sort of thing.'

Positive confrontation is saying what you want, rather than what you do not want. For example, 'I want you to get your next three reports in on time', rather than 'Your next three reports must not be late.' For other examples, see the chart on page 110.

Confrontation

Negative	Positive
I think you're obstructive.	I want constructive criticism.
I dislike you always being late.	I need you to arrive on time.
I consider you talk too much.	I want you to listen more.
I find your reports too long.	I need shorter reports.

Step 1 Say clearly what you want:
'I'd like you to listen more and be more constructive.'

Step 2 Explain clearly what effect the behaviour has on you or others:
'I find it insensitive when you keep interrupting.'

Step 3 Give a specific example:
'When John made his proposal you rushed in and rubbished it.'

Step 4 Ask for change:
'In our next meeting I'd like you to listen more and say how you can improve things, rather than producing negative comments.'

Plan when and where confrontation will occur. For instance, before the meeting, think about what the person does well, such as making good sales presentations, developing leads, attending to detail. Find recent examples to show these in action. Even if you never use them, it reminds you that the person makes positive contributions too. Similarly, be ready with specific examples of the behaviour you find unacceptable.

It often makes sense to take the person aside, rather than confront them in public. This saves their face and gives them a chance to acknowledge their behaviour and indicate that they will try to act differently.

If you intend doing it in your office, greet the person pleasantly when they arrive and step from behind your desk. Smile and say something friendly, like 'Thanks for coming. Let's both sit over here.' You will probably do this anyway if you are an outgoing person. Give some thought to the seating arrangements. Desks or tables create a communication barrier between people. Sitting next to someone, side by side, makes it harder for them to be aggressive and confrontational back. However, be careful to allow them sufficient physical space from you.

People often already know that their behaviour is causing problems. Even if this is a confrontation session, at least give them the chance to acknowledge that there is a problem. So, for instance, ask if they think any areas in their performance need changing, or if they know what you are currently concerned about. If they mention their problem behaviour, start discussing the changes you want. If they do not mention it, say directly what you want. Maintain eye contact, without glaring. Wait for their reaction, and if necessary ask for a response.

Use fact-seeking questions to discover whether the person sees any problems in achieving what you want, questions like: 'What do you need to do it that way next time?' Use open ended questions to encourage them to talk about the issue, For example, 'What do you think of your tendency to keep interrupting other team members?'

Ask the person to summarise the conversation at the end. Check that they have heard and interpreted it correctly, including the agreed action.

Dismissal

You cannot easily dismiss someone without a cost to you or the organisation. For example, there are increasingly tough employment laws that may make it expensive to take this action. Moreover, you can seldom continue firing people without affecting your reputation as an effective manager of people. At some point, you will be stuck with someone whose problem behaviour must be managed.

The Case for Firing

Organisations differ considerably in what behaviour they consider justifies firing. Broadly, however, it is probably justified for:

- dishonesty, which might include lying, making derogatory remarks about you behind your back or persistently running down the organisation when talking to other employees
- excessive absenteeism
- substance abuse
- lack of co-operation – flatly refusing to carry out instructions, persistently ignoring instructions and proceeding with their own methods without first checking their acceptability, complaining to the person above their own line manager without first confronting the line manager
- lack of productivity

Managers are sometimes surprisingly reluctant to take the final step, rightly feeling that dismissal is a reflection on their own ability to manage. It is emotionally hard and one may feel:

- guilty
- reluctant to tell the bad news
- worried about the legal ramifications
- concerned that it will be hard to find a replacement.

While these are understandable, they can prevent a rational decision that is in the interests of the organisation, and perhaps of the person themselves.

Do not immediately assume that direct dismissal is necessary. By negotiating with the person, exploring how they see the options, you may find that they themselves suggest a parting of the ways, perhaps after an agreed period of time. If you intend to deal with a difficult employee through dismissal:

- Seek professional advice on the best way to do it. There may be specific organisational rules for issuing a series of warnings before you are empowered to take this course of action.

- Explore the termination options with the employee.

- Reduce the possibility of legal action with sound documentation. Keep records of warnings, detailed information on failures to perform or other adverse behaviour. Keep the person's appraisal record up to date.

- Be willing to stick to your guns. Dismissal in large organisations and public agencies can take quite a time.

- Be prepared for the 'reverse sympathy' phenomenon. While you are dealing with the problem behaviour you may receive plenty of sympathy about your difficulties. Once you begin the dismissal process, however, you may end up being seen as the villain.

- Try not to take the whole process too much to heart. It is not a light hearted matter to dismiss a problem employee, but it does not have to be personally destructive either. The unpleasantness will pass.

Further reading

HONEY P. *Improve Your People Skills*. London, IPM, 1988

HONEY P. *Problem People*. London, IPM, 1992

12 *twelve*

Team Briefings

In Roman times, it took only a few hours for a message from a general to reach every single centurion. Team briefings have a long, respectable history, and are essential for running any effective organisation. They are a vital management skill and an increasing number of enterprises expect their executives to be good at them.

With teams becoming a pervasive way of organising work, being a good team briefer means learning the skills to do it with confidence. An essential difference between the days when Roman generals used team briefings and the modern era, is that today's briefings tend to be more of a two-way affair. They are not merely about cascading information downwards, like tablets from the mountain. They are also concerned with funnelling information upwards, so that decision and policy makers are better informed about what they are doing.

In fact briefings are a valuable management tool only if they are not passive, and everyone has an opportunity to contribute.

New Listening

The Industrial Society conducted a survey among 1,000 managers in 1994. They rated team briefings as the best method of communicating with their work force and hearing staff views.

Asked to nominate the most effective way of communicating with employees, over half (57 per cent) of the managers nominated team briefings. The next most effective channel, large staff meetings or 'road shows' scored only 11 per cent.

The briefing was rated as the best way of getting opinions from employees, ahead of the next most effective method, 'walking the job'.

Team briefings can play an important part in contributing to the way the organisation manages its future. Information from these meetings may enable you help the organisation think, plan and achieve its longer term strategic intent. For example, what do those who take part in such briefings think about what customers will want in the future? What ideas do they have for maintaining and enhancing the organisation's competitive edge? Often the answers to these questions seem highly parochial. People only know about their team, their own jobs, their local situation. By giving people the wider context you help them contribute to making the organisation adaptable and able to re-define its future.

Team briefings are a way of bringing everyone together to share information. In theory you can hold a team briefing over the telephone, through video conferencing and even by computer networking and soon perhaps virtual reality. However, the essence of an effective briefing is having everyone actually in the room at the same time, talking face to face.

The briefing is not an occasion for chastising people. It is not a disciplinary session or an opportunity to put people in their place. If people leave feeling blamed, then the session has been a failure. It is an extension of the regular team meeting, and if you do not have these it is time to start them. The briefing session you call is yet another way of building your team, strengthening relationships and enhancing collaborative working.

Some organisations (Federal Express, for instance) make team briefings into planned and regular events. Everyone expects a team briefing at known intervals. They are also meant to run in a certain predetermined way.

Briefings in Federal Express

The company's in-house guide explains that a team briefing is:

- a half hour meeting
- to allow two-way communication
- held monthly and in company time
- with dates displayed in advance
- led by the work group leader
- monitored by the work group's manager.

Content:

- core brief
- contract information
- work group information
- performance measures.

Regularity lets you make the team briefing system work for you. It gives everyone plenty of opportunity to learn how to use the time constructively. It also also gives you practice.

A football team that only meets once a season with its coach would not do particular well in matches. Sports teams hold regular briefings both before and after each game and business teams need to do the same. Choose appropriate events to trigger a briefing session.

Ask people to reserve specific dates in their diaries for regular team briefings. This allows them to plan their own time well and underpins the principle of regularity.

Regular briefings are not the same as frequent ones. For example, you could hold a regular team briefing only twice a year, which would hardly be frequent. Most teams require a formal briefing at least once a month, others more frequently. The nature of the issue and the sort of team dictates how often you should call briefings. Avoid calling one when you have nothing worthwhile to say. There needs to be a significant issue that is worth sharing.

While there is no maximum time limit to a successful briefing, the best ones are usually reasonably short, probably no more than an hour or 90 minutes, often a lot less. Beyond an hour, people generally start to lose concentration. Moreover, most people's memories are only able to recall about half a dozen key points, so extending the time is not necessarily helpful. So keep briefings short and involving, rather than long and passive.

Conducting a briefing

Preparation

Briefings put you centre stage, where people expect and want you to shine. This is another reason for preparing carefully. Just as some talented actors can occasionally get away with not bothering to rehearse or learn their lines, you may be able to get away with improvising. But it is risky, and while it may work a few times it is definitely not the best way to become an effective team briefer.

The preparation required for gaining everyone's attention is similar to what you would do for making any verbal presentation (see Chapter 15). For a start you need to be absolutely clear about the purpose and the message you want to get across.

An effective way of starting to make briefings work is to ask yourself:

● What is the main headline I want them to remember?

Headlines

Sum up the briefing message in a single sentence, perhaps a few key words:

- tighter budgets
- fewer jobs
- a product breakthrough
- a new deadline
- handling the new contract.

When you are absolutely clear about what message you want to communicate people will notice your confidence and respond accordingly. If you are full of 'ums' and 'ers' and wander from one point to another without any sense of purpose the briefing is unlikely to be effective.

Making an impact

Beyond sound preparation and being clear about the main message there are certain basic principles worth following. The first is:

- Be specific.

People do not want waffle with a kernel of information buried inside. Give specific information, with examples and facts, rather than generalisations. For example, if the purpose of the briefing is to tackle a newly imposed deadline, say so. Avoid a lengthy explanation about market forces, pressures on top management, technical considerations and so on.

Constantly referring to events outside your control merely emphasises a sense of powerlessness. What people want from the briefing is a specific picture of what has changed, what is going to happen, and what they can do next.

The second principle is:

- Explain the purpose of your briefing.

If necessary give people the headline, the one-liner that sums up everything. It may seem too direct, but most people welcome openness.

Thirdly:

- Break the information into manageable chunks.

This allows people to absorb it more easily. Since people can only remember a few key points from any lecture or talk, there is little point in cramming the time with endless facts and detail. Give them digestible amounts.

To the Point

- Be specific rather than general.
- Explain the precise purpose of the briefing.
- Start with a short overview of the whole message.
- Break information down, so that people receive the most important facts first.
- Reduce the message to no more than seven points.
- For each point, explain its importance to:

    the team
    the individual team member
    you the leader
    the organisation
    other parties

- Say what will happen next.

Fourthly:

- Spell out the implications.

This means you should answer the hidden question everyone is silently asking: 'What does this mean for me?' You may need to cover the implications for the team, the individual team members, the team leader, the organisation and other affected parties such as clients, trade unions or shareholders.

Finally:

- Say what will happen next.

State what you think will occur, such as a changes in work schedules, a programme of redundancies starting next month, a switch in priorities from one area to another and so on. If you do not know exactly what the implications are, say so. People generally react more favourably to someone who explains the limits of their present knowledge.

Be careful not to dump your own anxieties on the rest of the team. For example, if you are giving people bad news, try to avoid appearing as if you are blaming other people, or feeling helpless. This makes you seem more a victim than a manager.

Involvement

Well run briefings give people a chance to get involved. They need to be two-way affairs, with people asking questions and discussing the new situation. Inexperienced managers are often disconcerted by the apparent lack of response from the team. People may sit there looking blank, nobody comments, there may not even be any questions.

Silence does not mean the briefing has failed. People may still be trying to make sense of what they have heard. Also, if there are more than three or four people in the room, some people may be reluctant to talk.

Keep the task of giving information to about half or two thirds of the total time available. Leave the remainder for people to start processing the information and offer their reactions.

Consider calling a short break after the formal provision of essential information. Ask people to discuss what they think about what they have heard, with a colleague or in small groups. This gets people talking and breaks the stilted silence that may have arisen. After a few minutes ask the pairs or small groups to sum up their thoughts in a few sentences and to choose someone to convey them to the rest of the meeting. This will almost certainly raise plenty of questions or issues.

A prompt start

Because they know that briefings are important, most team members will arrive on time. You can encourage them to do so by asking people to come ten minutes early in order to socialise and have refreshments.

If people arrive late, do not reward them by starting your briefing all over again. Make a point of welcoming their arrival and suggesting that they talk to a colleague afterwards to catch up on what they have missed.

Materials

Team briefings are essentially about face-to-face contact. Since some people absorb information better if they have something in writing, consider giving a one page summary of the contents of the briefing. Only occasionally is the information too sensitive to handle in this way.

Take careful notes of any questions since these may be useful to share with other decision makers. They may also remind you that certain issues need to be followed up with giving people more information.

When you are being briefed

Often you will receive a briefing that forms the basis for your own team briefing. On behalf of your team you need to think of questions they might want answered, to challenge assumptions or to explore the implications of certain decisions.

Go to your own briefings as an ambassador or representative of your team. Take notes if the issue is complex and find out exactly what you can tell your team. For example, how much of your own briefing is confidential, and how much may be shared?

When you brief your team assume that nothing will remain confidential for long. Keeping secrets in most organisations is simply impossible. So treat all your team briefings as if it was being widely broadcast. This may seem an extreme case of mistrust or paranoia, but practical experience suggests that most team briefings leak.

Further reading

LEIGH A. and MAYNARD M. 'How to Lead and Inspire a Team' in *Leading Your Team*. London, Nicholas Brealey, 1995

13 *thirteen*

Project Management

Despite careful planning and the king's own close interest, plus plenty of resources, the Great Pyramid was at least a year behind schedule. The cost of the Channel Tunnel escalated way beyond the original estimates and it too was finished much later than intended. Not much seems to have changed in several thousand years.

At some time most managers have to lead a project and need basic project management skills. Nowadays, unlike Egypt's pharaoh, you can call on some important new techniques. However, as the Channel Tunnel shows, having them available is not quite the same as making them work for you.

What exactly is a project? The international consultancy firm Coopers and Lybrand, which lives or dies by the success of its projects, has a simple, two-line definition:

- a programme of work to bring about a beneficial change, with finite constraints of time, cost and quality.

The concept of a project applies to an enormous range of industries, circumstances and business situations. Yet behind the diversity is a common approach and a set of common principles that most managers can learn and use when necessary.

Businesses are increasingly turning to project management in one form or another to tackle difficult tasks. Traditional structures are often not ideal for bringing new products to market quickly or solving difficult technical problems.

In the wider context of the organisation's longer term future, project management may play a critical role. There may be a multitude of projects that together help it solve important strategic problems and redefine its future.

However, there is a limit to the number of projects an organisation can create and control. One of the limitations is available resources, another is time. Choose carefully what you use project management for. Because it can handle a great deal of complexity, it is often best used in areas of strategic concerns, such as helping to define the future.

Benefits of project management:

- Draws on wide ranging skills
- Shifts focus to linked objectives
- Tackles complexity and other pressures
- Increases the focus on business aims
- Is driven by a clearly identified person
- Recognises the human and technical aspects
- Is proactive and forward looking
- Recognises uncertainty and risk
- A useful learning arena.

The 10 commandments of project management

Project management is so well established that there are now some fairly reliable guidelines on how to make it work well. While project management arrangements differ widely, the basic principles are widely known. You could call them the 10 Commandments of project management.

1 *Projects are there to achieve a specific purpose.* Unlike a committee or even a long standing team, projects are usually focused on a highly specific goal. They do not exist for their own sake but in response to a particular organisational need.

2 *Every project needs a customer.* There needs to be a person or group of people who strongly desire the result of the project. This is the owner or sponsor.

3 *One person needs to be in charge.* The project leader is responsible for results and needs to have the ability to deploy the necessary resources to ensure success.

4 *The principles and policies underpinning the project should be spelled out at the start.* Clarifying everything from the brief to the reporting system is essential for a well run project.

5 *Planning needs to be in terms of tasks and people.* Identify the detailed project activities, and who is responsible for what.

6 *Have a system for controlling the project.* The history of project management is full of disasters where, despite a horde of experts and specialists employed to check on progress, expenditure went haywire and timing went out of the window.

7 *The project team needs to be carefully chosen.* Project members should represent the necessary skills and have access to resources. A project without the right people will fail.

8 *Create an agreed system for regularly reporting progress.* It does not have to be elaborate. It does need to be regular and understandable. Yards of computer print-outs are no substitute for basic information about whether the project is on time, on budget and on target.

9 *Make realistic estimates of completion time.* Estimates are essential, but they are only approximations. The more complicated the project the harder it is to meet the vast number of completion dates. Once slippage occurs it tends to reverberate throughout the project and bringing it back on line can be difficult. Good project managers always insist on building in plenty of slippage time.

10 *Projects need a defined beginning and ending.* Clarify the exact start and end dates so that everyone concerned understands the time boundaries. Prepare people for the ending date and make sure the project is wound up, not allowed to drift on.

Setting up

Adopt a project management approach if the task has a wide scope, much of the territory to be covered is unfamiliar, the issues are complex and a great deal is a stake. Project management is expensive and needs to be used with discrimination.

The secret of selecting a project manager is not to be blinded by a person's apparent brilliance at the purely technical aspects of project control. Someone who keeps wonderful progress charts, who documents everything meticulously and who has a passion for order may seem to be the ideal person. Yet successful project management is not just about order and control.

Good project managers know how to get the best from people. They are effective team workers themselves. They realise that no matter how well the project is monitored and documented, what will make it a success is the people involved.

The 10 Commandments listed above are a useful guide in establishing a project, and No. 3 (having one person in charge) is particularly important. Whenever you create a project team make sure that you clearly designate who will lead it and what resources they control.

The project manager must be able to challenge the assumptions and targets of people, departments, customers etc. especially when the project team is drawn from a variety of sources and members have mixed loyalties. You can therefore help the project leader in handling this challenge by the way you set up the arrangements in the first place. For example:

- Give the project team full responsibility for doing the total job.

- All project team members should report to the project leader while they are on the project team. If the project work runs parallel with their normal work clarify how people's priorities are to be decided.

- Ensure that everyone joining the project team clearly understands the task and the team's responsibilities. It may be necessary for you to meet the team members personally and brief them on their contribution.

- Keep the project team stable by not allowing members to be drafted to do other work that undermines their project responsibilities.

- As the project sponsor or champion, find a way of giving the team feedback on how you see its efforts and its progress so far.

Keeping track of a project

Projects consist of a set of activities or tasks to be completed. These can usually be broken into sub-activities. Complex projects such as building a new airliner consist of thousands of separate activities that start as broad brush ones: build the fuselage, design the wings, create the cabin interior. Each is then broken down into hundreds of other tasks.

Most people can only comprehend about 10 or 20 activities before excess detail blurs the sense of what is happening. Keep the number of main activities to a manageable number, usually around 6–15. These may then be further subdivided as separate sub-projects.

Networks

Networks are a graphical way of showing you the entire project, while also revealing the way activities relate to each other. Producing a network allows you to examine all parts of the project and analyse its constituent parts. This way you can decide both what needs to be done and in what order. There may be many possible ways to sequence the work and by viewing the interdependencies you can choose the most effective one.

The sequence of activities that completes the project in the least time is called the *critical path*. Any delay in completing the tasks on this path will cause the project to be delayed.

In many projects you can vary the amount of time allowed for certain activities, and the network enables you to see the effect of altering some of these. Nowadays most project managers rely on a computer to calculate the critical path and draw the network.

Computers

Spread sheets were once used to keep track of large scale projects. Nowadays there are specialist computer packages that list, track, and report on project activities. Today these low cost project management packages are readily available and relatively easy to learn. They make the project manager's job much easier.

For computerised packages to succeed you need to give attention to:

● *Planning.* The project needs to be organised, logical and efficient. It is necessary to think in detail about it before it starts and a computer can help create a comprehensive and disciplined approach in preparing the project plan.

● *Monitoring.* This needs to be in sufficient detail and time for a clear picture of the status of the project to be seen. The package is a tool for data collection and fast presentation in table or graphic form. The main problem to watch for is an excess of information that no one can really absorb.

● *Control.* Adjustments to the project plan need to be made regularly and the package allows them to happen quickly.

● *Cost information.* Accurate and comprehensive cost information lies at the heart of many successful projects. The package system allows a rapid assessment to be made of the cost position at any stage.

● *Communication.* Information needs and flows should be considered at an early stage. The package is invaluable for producing such information quickly and visually.

Most packages calculate a critical path showing the fastest and most sensible route through all the many activities to completion of the project. Other facilities include creating Gannt or Project Evaluation and Review charts (PERT). All systems worthy of the name show, for each project activity, the earliest start date, the latest start date, which resources are over or under used and the estimated finishing time.

Many packages also offer a 'what if' facility. You can therefore explore the possible consequences of different actions on the final timing of the project. For example, you can calculate the impact of an overtime ban or a series of machine breakdowns.

Responsibilities chart

It often pays to produce a visible record of who is taking on what responsibilities in the project. This is sensible when you are trying to co-ordinate the inputs from different departments, suppliers or other outsiders. A responsibility chart is a useful way of establishing commitments and it is usually done by showing activities or tasks against named individuals. It should define who will:

- carry out the work
- take decisions alone
- take decisions jointly ·
- manage progress
- have to be consulted before a decision or action
- have to be informed before a decision or action
- be available for advice and tuition
- provide detailed help with a task.

Once the main responsibilities have been allocated, an effective project manager will ensure that people have a thorough understanding of what to do. This means breaking the project down into suitable task groups and individual activities.

Individual tasks should be broken down into sufficiently small divisions to enable people to have a weekly set of activities. With inexperienced project members it is sensible to ensure that they only have one thing to complete at a time.

Reporting

Most projects have a sponsor who expects to be kept informed about progress. The project team also needs information on how it is doing. Ideally there should be a report at least every two weeks, although this will depend on the type of project. Reports with too much detail delivered weekly are soon consigned to the bin. Useful ones focus on general progress, with differences between actual and expected progress. If the end date of the project is under threat this needs to be made clear. Good reports go further than just a list of what is on or off schedule. They also identify any actions needed to correct variances and show what the cost will be in terms of time and money.

The project manager

Systems do not manage projects – people do. They do it by making decisions and initiating action. Good project managers can handle complex, costly projects, working to tight deadlines. They usually have special qualities of technical know-how, decisiveness, calmness under pressure and diplomacy. The following list shows the main responsibilities of a project manager.

What project managers do:

- complete a feasibility study
- prepare the project plan
- define the work, time and cost forecasts
- manage the project's progress
- deal with the team relationships
- report back to the project sponsor
- manage the sponsor's expectations
- produce, through the team, the project results.

Because the project may cut across many organisational, geographical and even cultural boundaries, the project manager may need to handle situations where personal authority is uncertain or ambiguous. This means being able to handle conflict. The main sources of conflict are:

- project priorities
- schedules
- administrative procedures
- technical issues
- deployment of human resources
- relationships
- cost.

You should deal with these not by pushing them out of sight, but by forcing them out into the open.

Conflict situations are vigorously debated in a spirited, reasoned way, usually led by the project manager. The latter will stress the need to examine the evidence and resolve the issue quickly. Effective project managers also know the three Cs:

- consultation
- co-operation
- compromise.

Being appointed a project manager is usually a great compliment, even if it is a bed of nails. Once in the role you may not receive the sort of management support you expect and your relations with previously friendly colleagues may deteriorate as you drive forward to completion. Many managers have brought their project to a satisfactory conclusion but found themselves out of a job at the end. The pace is demanding, and once you have fulfilled the role it may be hard to slow down again, or revert to a more leisurely style.

Further reading

ANDERSON E. et al. *Goal-directed Project Management*. London, Kogan Page, 1984

14 *fourteen*

Leadership

What is the difference between a manager and a leader? This question now concerns many organisations and certainly matters to you too. Seeing yourself as a leader could be the single most important factor distinguishing you from other managers, with whom inevitably you are competing.

It is not always easy to define what separates management from leadership. But the basics are certainly clear. Leaders go beyond 'managing' or coping. They do more than simply respond to events, they shape them. While managers happily follow procedures and do what is expected of them, leaders create or redesign the rules. They do the unexpected. When you act as a leader you take responsibility for the future by trying to define how it will look.

A widely accepted view of the difference is that while managers 'do it right' leaders 'do what is right'. This is not simply splitting hairs. Leaders challenge procedures, question why things must be done in a certain way, and are prepared to act on the basis of what they think will best serve a particular goal, support a particular vision or underline a cherished value. While managers can be leaders and vice versa, the best managers actually *think* of themselves as leaders – and behave accordingly. The place where you might be most expected to show leadership qualities is when managing a team of people.

You are a manager when you handle day to day operations and see that they are efficient. In that sense you are like a maintenance engineer, seeing that everything works smoothly and faults in the system are ironed out quickly. You are a starting to be a leader when you regularly think strategically. This means discovering or helping to define the organisation's aspirations and its strategic intention. Strategic thinking is partly what separates managers from leaders, since this activity is concerned with redesigning the organisation's future.

Leadership styles

Once, leading a team mainly meant giving orders, delegating and supervising people's work. The role was highly directive. Those on the receiving end were expected to follow orders and do as they were told. This leadership approach was autocratic. It was task orientated, focused almost exclusively on results. It assumed that you could not trust people and that getting things done through others was a scientific discipline that could be tightly defined.

The alternative approach is more democratic. The leader uses participation to get things done, and is concerned to build relationships and morale.

For many years people saw the two approaches as incompatible, but, today there is realisation that different leadership styles can work in different circumstances, although some work better and more consistently than others. Rather than focusing on something as vague as leadership style, give your attention to your leadership behaviour.

Leadership behaviour tends to be broadly directive or supportive. When you are being directive you:

- set goals and objectives
- organise people's work
- assign priorities and decide the deadlines
- clarify roles
- show or tell people exactly how to do a job.
- constantly check whether people have performed.

Leadership behaviour is now moving away from such highly directive forms of behaviour. Instead it is becoming more supportive:

- focused on getting the best from people
- inspiring people to produce outstanding results
- encouraging tightly defined standards in terms of quality or getting it right first time.

Supportive leaders listen to their followers, regularly praise them and seek their ideas. They share the bigger picture and readily disclose information. This form of leadership is not just about problem solving together, it enables people to seek their own solutions.

In real life, effective leaders achieve a personal balance between being directive and supportive. Nowadays the resulting balance would be described as one's leadership style. Successful leaders adapt their approach to suit the particular occasion or situation. Having a choice of how to lead greatly expands your leadership impact. Instead of always responding predictably to situations, you can be more flexible, choosing behaviour that matches the current need.

Your adaptability may well determine the team's success. For example, if you are someone who always approaches situations systematically, there may be occasions when you would get a better result by relying more on intuition. The differences between these two approaches can be seen in the chart below. Achieving the right balance between being systematic and intuitive is another example of how leaders adjust their personal style.

Systematic Leaders:	Intuitive Leaders:
• make choices using a logical sequence of steps • justify decisions by evidence • identify constraints • emphasise the need for information • hate relying on guesses or gut reaction.	• jump from one logical step to another, then back again • avoid specifics while visualising the total situation • continuously redefine problems • justify decisions by results • rapidly explore and drop alternatives • follow instinct, and often act impulsively.

You can learn to be more adaptable by practising seeing what is required, using your repertoire of responses and improvising. You can do this by constantly reviewing what is happening in your team, and demanding and giving feedback. This is not the same as checking whether work is completed on time.

The ability to see what the particular situation demands sets leaders apart from managers, distinguishes inspiring leaders from pedestrian ones and contributes to that ill-defined factor, charisma. Charismatic leaders convince you that they really understand what is needed.

People vary in the amount of support they require from their leader. A recently formed team, for example, with inexperienced members, may need far more help focusing on direction than an experienced one. The maturity of those you are leading is a useful guide to how much support and direction they may need. Maturity in this sense does not depend on chronological age, but on the person's stage of development. You can broadly summarise the choice of leadership behaviour as shown in the chart below.

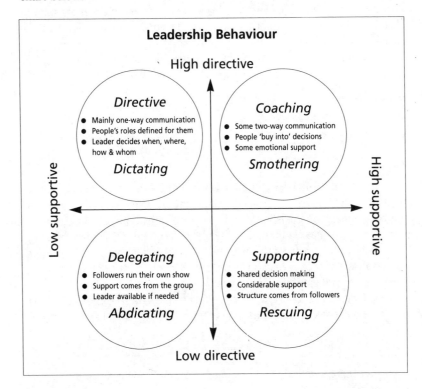

Motivation

Most people want to do a good job, and the challenge is to help them do it. People will only commit to important goals if they are really convinced about them, and want to make them happen. You cannot achieve that kind of commitment by orders, delegation and close supervision. Instead you must rely on tapping into people's natural wish to do something well. They will do so only if they feel they have some control over their lives. Instead of being told what to do, they learn for themselves their own power to make things happen.

We tend to think that motivating people is something one does to them. In fact the essence of motivation is discovering what people need in order to release their inner wishes. Leaders discover what 'turns people on'. To do this, all you have to do is ask them. It really is that simple. Spend time learning what excites them, what makes them tick, find out what they need in order to perform well. As managers, we are often so busy that we forget the value of spending time with people to establish what they require to perform well. We often take it for granted that simply paying them to put in an appearance at work is the same as motivating them. It is not.

There are some well established principles, derived from psychological research, for unlocking people's motivation. They are:

● goals
● expectations
● rewards.

Goals

People generally enjoy reaching for goals. The harder the goal, the more it tends to lead to better performance. Managing by objectives is one practical application of using goals to tap into people's motivation (see Chapter 1).

Setting goals has its limitations, however, especially if you are handing them out like tablets from the mountain. It is generally better, for example, to encourage people to establish their own goals with your help, rather than imposing them without discussion.

People need to know how they are doing in relation to the goals. How you give feedback is almost as important as the feedback itself.

Effective Feedback Is:

descriptive, non-judgemental, objectively describing what is happening

specific, avoiding generalities

relevant, providing what the receiver needs at that moment

timely, arrives when it is needed

usable, concerned with things or events over which the receiver has some control.

Feedback can be positive – encouraging – or negative – discouraging. Use negative feedback sparingly.

Expectations and rewards

Another important way of tapping into people's enthusiasm and commitment is to understand and use their expectations. When you ask someone to do something at work, their response may depend on how they expect these questions to be answered:

- If I try doing what you want, will I succeed in doing it?
- If I do it correctly, will it actually lead to a reward?
- Is the reward worth having?

To learn the answers you need to be willing to listen carefully to what people seem to want. Rewards mean different things to different people. To some it is a pay rise, to others it is time off or simple encouragement. Effective leaders learn to judge what rewards people need and then provide these. Two main types to consider are:

- intrinsic rewards
- extrinsic rewards.

Intrinsic rewards make people feel good inside when they achieve a goal, excel or please you in some way. They are positive feelings such as pleasure, satisfaction, pride, contentment, feeling wanted and so on. Extrinsic rewards come from outside the person, and include pay, bonuses, a company car, longer holidays, enhanced pensions, trips abroad and promotion. Poor leaders tend to rely too much on extrinsic rewards, often ignoring the power that intrinsic rewards have in gaining people's commitment.

Inspiration

Inspiring people is an important leadership quality that you can learn. You do not necessarily need to be a born leader to inspire people. But what does inspiration mean? A more popular word now used is empowerment. Both terms imply that you enable other people to do something exceptional.

Inspired people surpass themselves, going beyond their normal limits. They feel empowered to use their full potential, to give of their best. The best way to inspire people is to become inspired yourself. For instance, what makes you excited, energised, enthused, willing to go that extra mile? What is it about what you and your colleagues are trying to achieve that is so worthwhile? Can you explain this to the other people?

Leaders convey excitement, making people feel part of an adventure or a worthwhile journey. It is their own excitement, enthusiasm or commitment that stimulates people's wish to be part of what is happening. While charisma is certainly important, it is a willingness to share what matters to you with other people that creates it.

From both research and the lengthy experiences of successful leaders it emerges that there are three essential requirements for sharing:

- sharing your vision
- sharing your values
- sharing your understanding of goals.

Sharing your vision

In a company, the leadership vision may be anything from being the world's most progressive health care provider to being the most innovative boat builder. In a team the leadership vision might be anything from inventing a cure for AIDS to creating a production line for making mobile phones that has virtually no failures. Your role as an effective manager and inspiring leader is to help people find the vision that inspires them and to steadily convert this into realistic programmes of action.

If people are to commit themselves to trying to realise this vision they usually like to feel that they have some choice in the matter. It makes sense to stay flexible, and to be willing to respond to their wishes to modify or enhance your own vision in some way.

A team or a company without a vision is like a house without a foundation. It may stay upright for a while, but in the longer term it will start to topple. By sharing your vision you begin building strong foundations for your team or company.

Sharing your values

Values hold a team, or indeed an entire organisation, together. They are 'what matters to us around here'. Effective leaders:

- identify and articulate the values
- explain how to turn values into practical action
- demonstrate values in action by their own behaviour.

Examples of team values include: giving customers what they want; honesty and integrity; getting it right first time; having fun; being first; openness; confronting issues. Think of a team you know well. What are its values? What seems to really matter to this team, what would the team members say really matters to them?

If you ask an effective leader team what the team's core values are, you will almost certainly get a comment that describes how the team should behave in some way.

Effective leaders help people turn the values into practical action. It is one thing for example, for a team to have a value like 'integrity', but how does this translate into everyday behaviour? People may need considerable guidance in interpreting a particular value to guide their own behaviour.

The best way to explain how a value turns into practical action is to model it. In effect, you are saying, 'Look at me, I'm demonstrating it right now.' People constantly look to leaders for confirmation that important values are strongly held and demonstrated daily. They will only believe in a value when a leader confirms it through personal behaviour rather than merely words.

Sharing your understanding of goals

You can never assume that everyone sees goals the same way as you. Start the process of gaining mutual agreement by explaining to people what *you* see as important goals. Be prepared to elaborate these goals in the face of questions, particularly from members of your own team. People cannot begin to 'buy into' goals unless they really understand what they mean, and what their implications are. Be willing, also, to let people refine your understanding of goals, once they hear them spelled out.

What is expected of you?

Given the above, what exactly do people expect from you? Surveys have been remarkably consistent about what people want from an organisational leader:

- honesty
- competence
- a forward-looking approach
- inspiration
- intelligence
- fair-mindedness

These are not only values, they are also forms of behaviour.

To lead people well you need occasionally to stand back from the daily pressures and review how both you and those working for you are doing. Old fashioned top down appraisals do not work when it comes to judging your leadership. Instead you will need to be prepared to receive 360-degree feedback – information from below you, from people at your level and from above (see page 23).

Leadership feedback is seldom comfortable – it is nearly always personally challenging. However, an increasing number of companies expect their organisational leaders and senior managers to receive such sensitive information. It is therefore sensible to seek it out yourself rather than wait for it to be imposed on you. You can hardly expect people to tell you to your face or in a signed memo what they think of your leadership. You will need to create some means by which they can express their experience of your leadership in an anonymous way.

Personal Leadership Feedback

To obtain 360-degree feedback about your leadership you may need to ask people to rate your abilities on these sorts of issues:

- providing a good flow of communication concerning group strategy, company strategy or performance and departmental performance targets
- being a good coach for developing personal abilities
- providing recognition and praise for good work
- offering constructive criticism and support
- being open and interested in suggestions for improvement and change
- generating a good sense of team work
- being concerned about people's future
- co-operating in inter-team working
- being a good network contact for achieving work related goals
- inspiring people to reach beyond their normal limits

Extracting a special effort

At some time every leader needs to call forth a special effort from the team. Why do some teams respond, while others refuse the challenge?

In asking for a special effort effective leaders realise that people respond to more than just facts. Facts may start the process, yet they seldom work alone. Leaders also appeal to people's feelings, not just the logical, rational part of themselves. Sharing your feelings about why a particular effort is needed may be difficult if you are traditional manager who believes that emotions are too messy to handle. It may even feel vaguely unprofessional to resort to using emotions to get what you want. But to convince people that they can go beyond their normal capabilities, to exceed even their own view of what they can do, you need to show how much you care about achieving the goal. It is the intensity of your caring that will convince people, along with the hard facts and evidence.

´ Experiment to discover what will call forth and sustain a short-lived outstanding effort in your particular team. Sometimes the team itself is your best tutor, with people being willing to explain what makes them able to make that special effort.

Delegation

The opportunities for traditional delegation, in which you simply hand out tasks, are declining as organisations achieve their goals in less hierarchical ways. Delegation takes on greater significance, since it is really about sharing your leadership power.

Managers are often more reluctant to hand over a role than a task. Delegation provides a vital, on the job, learning experience for which there is no substitute. You enrich someone's job by giving them new powers to perform differently.

Many organisational leaders, however, are reluctant to share their power through delegation. They fear that they will become less effective and lose control. Certainly delegating is risky. If you normally insist on and achieve high personal standards the idea of not obtaining these can be almost unbearable. But the risks are worth it.

Delegation Means Accepting

- a longer timescale for completing some tasks
- temporarily lower quality than you yourself could achieve
- reduced personal enjoyment from performing certain activities
- fewer chances to practise your skills.

To make delegation work people need to know what is expected of them. Although a written brief may be too cumbersome, it can help add clarity to what you expect from someone.

When to delegate is mainly a matter for your personal judgement. It may be particularly appropriate when the task is complex and needs breaking into smaller, more manageable chunks that use a wide range of skills. It is also appropriate when people are asking for more authority or showing potential for taking more responsibility. This is when you share some of your personal power and thus empower them to do more than they have previously done.

Another sign of the right time to delegate is when you are personally working too hard, perhaps taking work home several times a week. This is the moment to share the burden. However, you need to ensure that you are not merely dumping all your stress and overwork on the next person in line.

If you can see how a task could make a routine for others to complete, this is another indication that it is right to delegate. Most of all, the right time is when you see an opportunity to develop a person by providing them with an important challenge.

When to avoid delegating

When you delegate you are relying on the willingness and ability of others to do what you might normally do yourself. You need faith in them and their abilities. Avoid delegation if you cannot have faith in them or if the task is:

- vital, and only you can be sure it will be done in time satisfactorily
- highly confidential and it would be wrong to let anyone else do it
- something which requires sensitivity and understanding, and it would be inappropriate for others to substitute for you
- so vague and ill-defined that there is little chance of someone else performing it well.

10 ways leaders manage the future*

- They manage the dream – creating a compelling vision, defining reality.
- They embrace error, and are not afraid of making mistakes and admit them when they do.
- They encourage reflective talkback, welcoming personal feedback about themselves.
- They encourage dissent, welcoming contrary views and those who can distinguish between the expected and what is happening
- They possess the 'Nobel factor', exuding optimism, faith and hope.
- They understand the 'Pygmalion effect', expecting the best from people around them, stretching them without letting them fall too short too often.

* Adapted from *On Becoming a Leader*, by Warren Bennis (Hutchison Books 1989)

- They have, and use, instinct, a sense of where the culture is going to be, where the team must be if it is to grow.
- They see the long view and are patient.
- They understand the 'stakeholder symmetry', – knowing they must reconcile the competing claims of interested parties.
- They create strategic alliances and partnerships, seeing the world globally, knowing that there is now nowhere to hide.

Further reading

BENNIS W. *On Becoming a Leader*. London, Hutchinson Business Books, 1989

LEIGH A. and MAYNARD M. *Leading Your Team*. London, Nicholas Brealey, 1995

15 *fifteen*

Presentations

Your heart thumps, your mouth is dry, your hands are sweaty, and there is a nasty feeling in your stomach as if butterflies are doing aerial stunts. No, you are not having a heart attack: you are about to make a presentation.

That is how many people react to standing up in public and talking. You are not alone if that is how you feel. Plenty of professionals respond that way too, despite years of practice. As comedian Tommy Cooper once said, the main difference between the amateur and the professional is that the latter gets the butterflies to fly in formation.

Numerous surveys around the world show that people who succeed in business and organisations present and communicate well. It is such a core skill that nowadays almost everyone who aspires to be a manager or a leader spends time learning to present with impact.

You need good presentation skills for a myriad reasons, for example when you apply for a job, ask for a pay rise, seek support for a project, when you need to borrow money from the bank, when you run a team meeting. Presenting well can be a major asset in your life.

When you tap your natural ability to present you also contact your personal power. It is a way of becoming a more effective human being. Nor is it necessarily difficult. However, you do need to work at it, to get regular feedback on your performance and to keep reaching for another level of impact. With presentations you can always do better next time.

If you are already a good speaker you may be tempted to rely too much on verbal presentations. This is risky. There are many occasions when it is better to give a written presentation. If what you have to say can be communicated adequately without you being there, send a report.

Signs that a verbal presentation is needed:

- A decision is urgently required.
- You are asked to speak on a specific occasion.
- You have something to offer beyond the written word.
- The recipients need to hear from you in person.
- Your message is more likely to be accepted with you present.
- There are too many complex ideas to rely on a written document.
- Your message does not need a written document.

Being an effective presenter

Depending on the organisation, giving powerful presentations will mark you out as an effective manager. Increasingly organisations regard it as essential that their managers communicate well through formal presentations. Sometimes, however, companies become obsessed with presentation to the detriment of other managerial skills. IBM, for instance, was once renowned for being so passionate about presentations that people used to spend literally weeks preparing theirs. Some managers even had overhead projectors built into their desks.

In the context of the organisation's future, your presentations need to include the wider picture of where the organisation is going and how it is getting there. Many of the topics on which you present may initially seem to have little or no relevance to such strategic issues such as the organisation's long term future. But by constantly returning to this theme and giving your reports that special focus, you will set yourself apart from those with a lesser vision.

Of course, you may run the risk of being regarded as having your head in the clouds, of not being pragmatic or realistic. Others who pride themselves on being down to earth may openly or covertly attack you for the way your presentations always put the issue in a broader context. But that may be why you are eventually promoted and they are not.

Mental attitude

Managers often seem to suffer from two extremes of mental attitude towards presenting. The negative extreme is believing that you are a poor presenter. Constantly telling yourself you are not a good presenter sends a negative message to your subconscious. In fact, everyone can present well and you are no exception. Keep reminding yourself that you can do it, and that you know it is essential for succeeding as a manager or a leader.

The positive extreme is wrongly believing that you are a superb presenter. Over-confidence and an inability to realise that you are not performing well prevents you from learning from your mistakes. Instead you just plough on regardless, boring audiences or failing to grab their attention.

In both cases you need honest feedback on how you are really performing. Often people who think they are bad presenters are in fact quite good, and only need a little help and regular feedback to start delivering outstanding performances. Similarly those with an exaggerated view of their impact need a chance to check out reality and then start to focus attention on improvements.

Try keeping an impact log, a written record of how you performed in each presentation so that you can constantly review your own progress. For instance you might score yourself on:

● how well you prepared
● how clear you were about your purpose
● whether you spoke with conviction
● whether you really used your personality
● whether you handled questions well.

Ask other people to complete the ratings on your performances too.

Obstacles

Some common obstacles to being an effective presenter:

● the use of written notes
● visual aids
● body language
● sub-text
● waffle.

Using full, written notes will undermine your presentation. Most poor presenters rely on detailed notes, even scripts, to get their message across. Consequently they come across as stilted and boring. Notes are a security blanket. When you really know and care about what you want to say, notes soon take a back seat.

The trick with notes is reducing them to key words. Certainly write out your entire speech, but then practise it until you know it sufficiently well to identify the core phrases or words that remind you of each point. Only professional actors can make a natural-sounding presentation while reading from a full script.

Reduce notes onto small cards that are easily carried in your pocket. Audiences do not enjoy seeing a presenter arrive centre stage and produce large amounts of paper.

Visual aids can make or break your presentation. Some carefully chosen ones can have a huge impact. However, too many will leave your audience more confused than when you started. Stick to a few powerful, well designed ones. Make sure that they can be seen clearly by a short sighted, elderly man at the back of the room, who also wears under-powered glasses. That is, make the contents large, bold and simple. Remember that words are not visual aids. Pictures are. It is so easy now to produce professional looking aids that there is really no excuse for yours to look amateurish.

Many things can go wrong with visual aids. Flipcharts can appear torn, dirty or too small. Slides can be projected inverted or back to front. Film clips can break at the crucial moment. Expect the worst and be prepared for it.

Your body cannot keep a secret. Standing before an audience, your body gives many hidden signs about how you feel and what you are thinking. Audiences pick these up automatically. We are all experts in our own way in body language. Even highly competent presenters can undermine their impact by being unaware of what their body is doing while they are performing. The chart below shows the importance of non-verbal communication.

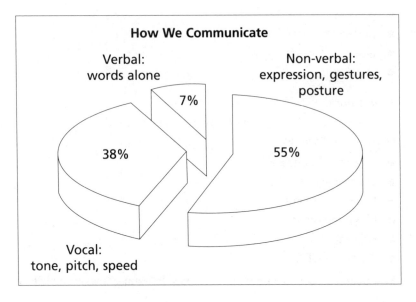

The two main ways of improving body language are:

● being thoroughly committed to a presentation
● obtaining regular feedback on your performance.

Use a video to have a look at yourself performing.

An audience has a sixth sense that identifies when a presenter is feeling nervous and it realises what is really being said 'between the lines'. What is being communicated *behind* your words is as important as the actual verbal content:

● Be clear about your purpose.
● Have a clear commitment to saying what you mean.
● Mean what you say.

Say what you have to say and then sit down. It is easy to ramble while presenting. Good presenters know if they have a tendency to waffle and rigorously try to curb it. They live by the actor's credo of leaving their audience wanting more. So say what you have to say . . . and then stop.

The five Ps of presentation

While there are many systems for making managerial presentations, the so-called five Ps have stood the test of time. They are:

● preparation
● purpose
● presence
● passion
● personality.

Preparation

Preparation includes everything you need to do in order to be ready to deliver your message:

● Research the audience.
● Devise the presentation.
● Organise the presentation aids.
● Check the venue.
● Rehearse.
● Ready yourself.

Researching your audience is one of the best investments you can make in becoming a better manager. Learning as much as you can about your target audience is a discipline that goes far beyond mere presentations. It is relevant to many other aspects of your work.

Researching your audience

- Who exactly is the audience?
- How many of them are there?
- What does your audience expect?
- Who might be talking before you?
- Are there any special factors that might affect your impact?

For example, does your audience need to be persuaded, amused, informed, challenged or what? Moreover, knowing that your audience will include, say, an assertive finance director who always demands hard financial evidence can help hone what you have to say to a fine edge.

There may also be some special factors to consider, such as knowing your audience is going to be anxious about what you have to say. For instance, if you are announcing increased profits and also plans for redundancies, your audience may not give you their full attention until you deal with the redundancy issue.

Preparation is also about constructing your presentation so that it flows smoothly and has a logical structure. The best-known framework is:

- Tell them what you are going to tell them.
- Tell them.
- Tell them again what you have told them.

Most good presentations have a definite beginning, middle and end.

The Five Steps to Creating an Instant Speech

Step 1 *Get attention.* Introduce your presentation with a catchy opening

Step 2 *Explain the relevance.* Tell your audience why the subject is important to them.

Step 3 *Present the central message.* Follow with a general statement of your purpose.

Step 4 *Give examples.* Support your message with some real illustrations.

Step 5 *Close.* End with a striking sentence that summarises your speech.

Preparation also means rehearsal. An audience soon detects when you have skimped on this. Even if you are good at improvising, good presentations are nearly always rooted in thorough rehearsal.

Purpose in performance

Apart from having a clear purpose when preparing your presentation, you also need to have a definite purpose *as you perform*. Throughout your presentation you need to be clear why you are saying what you saying. Why are you doing what you are doing and what effect do you want to achieve at any one moment? Knowing your purpose from moment to moment helps you vary the tempo, alter the attack and even your intonation. It also enables you to vary your range of expression.

Question time is a good example of purpose in performance. What exactly do you want to achieve in answering people's questions? This could be a great opportunity to expound your ideas and make them relevant to the audience. Regarding it as a threatening event in which people try to trip you up makes you act defensively.

Presence

Powerful presenters establish a presence. There is nothing mysterious about this and anyone can do it. It is all about being present in the moment, your entire attention concentrated on what is happening around you. Your senses are heightened, so that you notice things that you might normally miss.

For example, if you see a person at the far end of the table looking glazed, if you notice the room is a bit stuffy, if you hear the clicking of a keyboard just outside the room, then you are in tune with the moment. This alertness lets you respond instantly to signals from your audience.

An important way of establishing a presence comes right at the start of your performance. If you rush into your act the moment you are centre stage you do not give your audience time to absorb your arrival. Before you utter a word of your presentation:

- stop
- breathe
- look
- listen.

Allow a pause for five or more seconds before starting to speak. The power of this approach is considerable. It gives you time to 'arrive', to take in your audience and your surroundings. It also allows your audience time to absorb your arrival, assess your appearance, and to get comfortable with your being there.

Passion

Passion may seem a strange term in this context, but it is mainly about demonstrating your commitment to what you have to say. If *you* do not care about what you are saying, why should the audience? Your passion warms, excites, enthuses and holds your audience. When you are in touch with your passion you hardly need any notes; the words just come naturally.

If you are someone who is comfortable with facts, figures and analysis you may also be someone who thinks passion in presenting is irrelevant. Surely as long as you offer lots of evidence, people will be convinced. However, audiences vote with their hearts, not their heads. That is true even of top boards of directors or cynical investment analysts. Good presenters therefore create just the right level of involvement for their particular audience. They build a relationship with the audience.

Personality

It is your unique personality that will make your presentation memorable. Many people forget they have a personality when they present, and then wonder why they leave feeling that they have not done themselves justice!

Your personality makes your presentation different from anyone else's. What the audience wants is you, not an imitation of some well-known speaker or another senior manager. Try to let the real you come through when you present. Otherwise, you might as well just send them a report.

Ask friends or colleagues you trust, to give you feedback on how you come across on first impression. For example, they may highlight some simple distractions that detract from your ability to use your personality fully. These might include hair in front of your eyes, heavy make-up, pocket flaps askew, shoddy or creased clothes, tinted spectacles, keys jangling in your pocket.

Improving your presentation skills

You do not learn to ride a bicycle by reading about it. Likewise, you cannot speak a foreign language without practice. Good presentations also stem from plenty of rehearsal. Seek out plenty of live presenting opportunities and consider obtaining some formal training. Presentation workshops can be fun, and will point you in the right direction. They will identify your strengths so that you can begin using them more purposefully. They will also identify areas where you need to develop more. They offer a way of practising in a safe environment.

Also ask your own manager to comment on your presentations. Find out how important presentations are within the organisation and what help you might obtain to improve yours.

By choosing to improve your presentation impact, you will almost certainly impress those in positions of authority that you are serious about becoming a better manager.

Further reading

LEIGH A. and MAYNARD M. *Perfect Presentations*. London, Century Business, 1993

16 *sixteen*

Stress

How fast do you walk? The fastest walkers are the urban Japanese, followed by the Americans, Taiwanese and Italians. The slowest are the Indonesians. According to research from the Henley Centre, the richer you are the faster you live.

You not only walk faster, you also work longer, strive harder and suffer more *stress* in your attempts to become even richer, or maybe just to survive in modern society. Sneak a glimpse inside the desk of a random selection of top managers and, apart from the paper clips and notepads, you are almost sure to discover in some of them bottles and packs of pills for reducing stress.

Ashridge Management College found that three out of four managers see work as a source of stress, with women suffering more than men. Stress grows as you climb the ladder. Eighty per cent of board-level managers see work as stressful. In Britain, for example, half the company chairmen and chief executives in a survey by the University of Manchester suffered from work related stress.

Even if you are not a senior manager, stress can affect you and even kill you. The Japanese even have a word for it – *karoshi*, or death from overwork. Half of them live in fear of such a death. Heart disease is one well-known result of stress, but there are plenty of other symptoms, including depression, headaches, aggression and alcohol or drug dependency.

We tend to ignore the signs of stress as long as we can, sometimes too long. The early warning signs include tiredness, depression, inability to sleep and irritability. Next may come an inability to concentrate, job dissatisfaction, a low sense of personal achievement, and high rates of smoking, cholesterol or heart rate.

The impact of stress

To be a better manager, you need to handle stress for three reasons:

● your own health and effectiveness
● the health and effectiveness of your subordinates
● the impact on the organisation.

In the wider context of the future of the organisation, stress is an important issue of survival. When people are constantly stressed they may not think creatively about demanding issues to do with organisational vulnerability. Stress tends to force people and organisations to think short term and ignore the need to design and manage the future.

Yourself

It seems obvious that you should be concerned about the effects of stress on your own health and effectiveness. Yet a surprising number of managers, particularly at senior level, feel they are immune to stress or that they can readily cope with it. In fact the evidence is that you will reap the consequences of it in one way or another. It may be in terms of personal health and well being, it may be in terms of how you make decisions and your work in general.

Although many stress inducing factors are unavoidable, some can certainly be contained. The days of jobs for life are gone and you will be expected to be more flexible, adaptable and people orientated, but you can prevent stress from destroying your life and career if you take it seriously. Do so before it hits you, not afterwards.

Subordinates

You also need to be concerned about stress faced by your subordinates, because they are the people you depend on for your own success as a manager. If they succumb, your own effectiveness will be reduced.

You may feel that stress is no different from tension or pressure, and that it makes people more alert, competitive and efficient. You might argue, for instance, that some jobs, such as the emergency services or transport, are inherently stressful and if people choose to work in them they have to expect to handle stress.

In fact employees do not have an infinite capacity to take on more work in increasingly adverse conditions. Long and unsocial hours will take their toll. At one time, you could wait for an individual to crack, and then respond. This may no longer be good enough. In Britain, for example, you could be leaving your organisation vulnerable to an expensive legal claim for negligence.

The organisation

Apart from any possible legal implications of handling stress badly, the impact on the organisation can be widespread. People under stress affect others, and if you fail to deal with one case of stress you could be facing many others.

Stress reduces the organisation's ability to compete. For example, people may strongly resist change when under stress, new ideas may be rejected without proper consideration, important market opportunities may be missed.

Clients, customers and relationships may also be seriously affected when people are unduly stressed. The tactics that individuals adopt to handle stress may work for them, but the consequences for those around them are usually damaging. For example, when someone under stress starts working excessive hours, others may feel compelled to emulate them, with the result that work starts to become addictive. The cumulative effect may be to reduce everyone's efficiency rather than just one person's.

The causes of stress

An important reason for the high levels of stress that managers often experience is the steady increase in working hours. Over the last 20 years they have risen in the USA by the equivalent of one extra month a year. A similar pattern is emerging in Europe.

The extra hours result from flatter organisational structures with fewer managers working with fewer resources. In such circumstances people are expected to be more productive than ever. Widespread use of information technology continues both to eliminate the need for middle managers and to demand new technical skills.

Sources of stress at work:

- the changing management role
- the growing requirement to manage people and hence interpersonal relations
- organisational structure and climate
- career prospects
- the work and home interface
- conflict between being a specialist and a generalist

- conflict between being an individual and a team player
- inadequate support and recognition from one's boss
- relentless work pressure with little or no personal discretion
- poor work equipment and premises
- excessive organisational change
- fear of losing one's job.

While a limited amount of stress is certainly healthy, too much is damaging to you personally and to the organisation. Healthy stress keeps us alert and is the body's way of protecting us from potential dangers. It produces extra adrenalin, which temporarily stimulates greater energy and strength.

We all have some degree of stress tolerance and the point at which we begin to suffer serious damage can vary from one person to another. How stress affects you will depend on whether you are flexible or inflexible, introverted or extroverted and how well you fit into your job.

It is therefore partly up to you to learn how to spot the signs and act. Tension, fatigue, and irritability which lead to emotional detachment, withdrawal, cynicism and rigidity may be hard to catch early, and you may benefit from regular health checks as part of your determination to stay healthy.

Cost of Stress

The CBI has estimated that stress costs UK employers £4bn a year.

A study in the early 1990s by the Massachusetts Institute of Technology suggested that depression at work was costing the USA $47bn, much the same as heart disease.

Although one can list many potential causes of stress, the most fundamental reason may be ourselves. The way in which we interpret events around us may entirely determine whether we react to them in a stressed way or not. For example, if you are summoned to see the chief executive, having just made a mistake, you are hardly likely to interpret this as an occasion for rejoicing. When you get there, however, you may learn that the reason for the summons had nothing to do with the mistake at all.

Thus we view the world through our own screen and are affected by our own set of beliefs. It may not be the event at all that is causing the stress, only our interpretation of it. The chart on page 153 demonstrates this effect.

The ABC of Stress and Distress

(A) ─────────────► (B) ─────────────► (C)

Activating event   Beliefs   Consequences:

                            │   Mental (Self-talk)
                            ▼   Emotional (e.g. Anger)
                          We interpret the   Physical (Tension)
                          event according   Behavioural
                          to our view of
                          the world and of
                          ourselves.

The above shows the role of interpretation in stress.
While A is the stressful event or situation, B is how we
view it. C shows the mental physical, emotional and
behavioural consequences. Adverse consequences might
be anxiety, sweaty hands, smoking more than usual.
Favourable consequences might be positive
anticipation, a feeling of being stimulated and facing
an exciting challenge.
Event A does not directly cause C. Instead B, consisting
of beliefs about ourselves and other people, intervenes.
How we see the world may be just as important as how
the world actually is.

The consequences of stress

When you are stressed you are less effective as a manager. For example, the symptoms of tired behaviour are well known. You start to make things simpler just in order to keep functioning. You start polarising issues into black or white, right or wrong.

Under stress you may tend to start stereotyping people and situations to fit them into familiar boxes that you know how to deal with. You may shorten your time horizons and postpone all difficult decisions until another day. Or worse, you may make rushed, irrational choices.

When over-tired you may also tend to talk rather than listen, it helps to keep you awake. You may also find that emotion rather than reason is starting to take over and to keep going there may be a temptation to resort to drink or other stimulants.

The impact of stress on you may also be affected by whether you are mainly responsible for things or for people. Responsibility for people means constantly interacting with them, attending meetings and often working under pressure. Responsibility for people is also closely related to heavy smoking, raised blood pressure and so on. People who are mainly concerned with things on the other hand tend to be less affected by stress.

The way in which you are affected by stress will also depend on whether you are a Type A or a Type B person. The Type A person is typically extremely competitive, strives for achievement and may be aggressive, hasty, impatient, restless, very alert, with explosive speech and tense facial muscles, and may feel under pressure of time and the challenge of responsibility.

By contrast, Type B people tend to be more easy going, take difficulties in their stride, spend time on what they do, and maintain a careful balance between events and actions demanding their energy.

A Type A person is more likely to suffer heart disease than a Type B person. While you cannot readily alter your whole personality, you can at least be aware which type you tend towards and watch for the danger signs. For instance, Type A people tend to seem less interested in exercise and their general lifestyle leads to ill health.

There are various ways to assess your stress level at any particular moment so that you can take counter measures. For example the table on page 155 shows your chances of becoming ill due to stress in the next 12 months. Alternatively you can seek a regular medical assessment to gauge your fitness, blood pressure, cholesterol levels and so on.

Combating stress

While you should resist excessive amounts of work for yourself or your subordinates, this is less critical in causing stress than regularly working long hours. This upsets the all-important balance between work and private life.

If you or your subordinates are taking work home several nights a week, and frequently working more than 60 hours a week, it is time to act. Long hours do not necessarily mean you are being fully effective or productive. In Germany, for example, which has the most successful economy in Europe, managers typically work far shorter hours than in any other European country, particularly the UK. If a German boss sees a junior manager consistently working late he or she either thinks they are not coping, are not managing their time properly, or are insecure about their job. Cancelling holidays is regarded as seriously delinquent behaviour.

The secret of handling stress is to work better, not harder. You ought be able to increase your productivity by as much as 25 per cent through

The Stress 'League Table'

(For anyone scoring more than 300, a major illness can be predicted within one year for 80 per cent of individuals. All life events within the past two years qualify.)

Death of spouse	100	Trouble with in-laws	29
Divorce	73	Outstanding personal	
Marital separation	65	achievement	28
Jail term	63	Wife begins or stops work	26
Death of close relative	63	Begin or end school	26
Personal injury or illness	53	Change in living condition	25
Marriage	50	Revision of personal	
Dismissal	47	habits	24
Marital reconciliation	45	Trouble with boss	23
Retirement	45	Change in work hours	
Change in health of relative	44	or conditions	20
Pregnancy	40	Change in residence	20
Sex difficulties	39	Change in school	20
Gain of new family member	39	Change in recreation	19
Business readjustment	39	Change in religious	
Change in financial status	38	activities	19
Death of close friend	37	Change in social activities	18
Change of job	36	Mortgage or loan less	
Change in number of		than £8,000	17
arguments with spouse	35	Change in sleeping habits	16
Mortgage over £8,000	31	Change in number of family	
Foreclosure of mortgage	30	get-togethers	15
Change of responsibilities		Change in eating habits	15
at work	29	Vacation	15
Son or daughter leaving		Christmas	12
home	29	Minor violation of the law	11

proper time management (see also Chapter 17, on controlling your time).

It also means allowing space for a full private life. People are simply more productive when they have a life outside work. They are also more interesting and alive. However, going home to dump the stress on a partner who may also be facing stress, or to slump in front of the television, is not having an outside life. Merely going home and brooding about work will not contribute to reducing stress, it merely adds to it.

Some symptoms of stress are relatively easy to spot since they emerge as a lack of concentration, irritability, aggression and a failure to retain a sense of humour. These are all signs that you or a colleague are about to cross the divide between healthy pressure and stress. This is the time to fight the urge to go into the office at weekends, and instead take a day off.

Get right away from work so that you can take the pressure off while you adjust the balance. In Scandinavia, companies allow employees to take up to five 'mental health days' off a year. Instead of phoning up and saying you have flu, you say you are taking a mental health day.

You are unlikely to receive much help from your boss, who is probably also stressed. Although some companies offer executive counselling, most still treat stress as a dirty word. If you are going to combat stress and remain an effective manager, you will have to look after yourself and manage your own stress.

Stress busters

While you may not be able to avoid coming face to face with stress, you need not succumb to it. There are many personal and organisational strategies that you can adopt to eliminate it or at least reduce it to manageable levels.

Empowering others   An important step you can take is to empower others to extend their range of work, for example by encouraging them to widen their job, to make decisions previously taken by you, to take on new responsibilities. You need to resist that nagging fear that you will lose control.

Learn about managing people   If you have previously mainly managed things and are promoted to a job that involves managing people, this is a good time to seek some training. For example, consider asking for help in learning how to:

- unlock people's motivation
- deal with difficult employees
- cope with the resistance arising from managing change
- be a more effective communicator
- understand how to pass on work and issue instructions
- encourage participation.

Watch your diet   Stress quickly affects people's eating habits. For example, when you are stressed you may tend to eat too much or too little, skip breakfast, miss lunch and grab snacks along the way. Many managers enjoy feeling so busy that they cannot spare the time for lunch and if that is happening to you, take action. Count the number of times you have forgotten to take lunch in the last two weeks. If you have missed more than three or four lunch breaks, you have the first signs that you may be heading into excessive stress.

Dietary habits have long been known as important factors in causing stress, combined with smoking. The smoke-filled room, with plenty of pastries or biscuits and endless supplies of coffee, is potentially damaging to your well-being.

Relaxation   There are numerous ways in which you can seek to relax and combat the effects of work-related stress. If you have your own office, try closing the door and putting a notice on it saying you cannot be disturbed for 15 minutes. If possible, lock it too. Switch off the phones and any other device that could disturb you. Carry out the 10 steps to relaxation shown on page 158 and give yourself a break.

My own company regularly calls in a massage service which brings a special chair on which to sit and receive the treatment. Each person has about 15 minutes' massage, and we all return to work feeling re-energised and with a new sense of well-being.

One of the most powerful and well-established ways of combating the effects of stress is regular meditation. This is not something that only Indian gurus or adherents of strange sects do. Anyone can do it, and it is not complicated or difficult to learn. Meditation sessions can vary according to your particular need. A few minutes during the day can transform the way you handle your work. Fifteen minutes at the start of each day could alter your life. It is so effective that many companies have paid for their managers to learn to do it and you could explore whether yours will do so.

External relaxation also includes sport, hobbies and other non-work activities that absorb your time and interest. What is important is to eliminate work from your mind for long enough to give yourself a real break so that you return to it refreshed. When you do this your productivity is nearly always enhanced.

Helping others

If you manage other people you can help them cope with stress by encouraging them to develop personal strategies for dealing with it. Women in particular may need help to realise how much they are falling victim to stress. Often their stress stems from feeling a lack of control or power over their work environment. The chart on page 159 offers some specific suggestions for Type A women managers.

10 Steps to Relaxation

1 Sit in a comfortable chair, feet flat on the floor, with your eyes closed.

2 Become aware of your breathing.

3 Take in a few deep breaths. As you let out each breath, say to yourself mentally, 'Relax'.

4 Concentrate on your face. Feel any tension in your face and eyes. Make a mental picture of this tension – it might be a knotted rope or a coiled spring. Picture this relaxing and unwinding, growing looser and more comfortable, like a sack of wet sand.

5 Experience your eyes and face becoming relaxed. As they relax, feel a wave of relaxation spreading though your whole body.

6 Tense your eyes and face, squeezing them tightly, then relaxing them. Feel this same relaxation throughout your body.

7 Do the same with other parts of your body, squeezing and relaxing each part from your head to your toes, in this order.

jaw	chest
neck	abdomen
shoulders	thighs
back	calves
upper arms	ankles
lower arms	feet
hands and fingers	toes

Do this until every part of your body is relaxed. For each part of your body, mentally picture the tension, see it melting away.

8 When you have relaxed each part of your body, rest quietly in this comfortable state for two to five minutes.

9 Let the muscles of your eyelids slowly lighten up, become aware of your surroundings again, and prepare to open your eyes.

10 Now open your eyes. You are refreshed, and ready to resume your usual activities.

Reducing Stress for Type A Women Managers

- Try to control your obsessional time-directed life by making yourself aware of it and changing the established pattern of behaviour.

- Restrain yourself from trying to be the centre of attention by not constantly talking, particularly when there is no real need to do so.

- Develop reflective periods in your self-created hectic programme for life and assess the causes of your 'hurry' sickness.

- Most of your work does not require immediate action. Tell yourself at least once a day that no enterprise ever failed because it was executed too slowly, too well.

- Indulge in outside activities, theatre, reading, etc, to lessen obsessional, time-oriented behaviour.

- Try not to make unnecessary appointments and impossible deadlines.

- Protect your time; learn to say 'no'.

- Take as many stress free breathing spaces during the course of an intensive working day as possible.

- Try to create opportunities during the day or night when you can entirely relax your body and mind.

There are courses on handling stress that you might suggest to your subordinates if you notice that stress is becoming potentially damaging.

Teams are an excellent way of reducing stress by sharing anxieties and peer group support. If stress symptoms are arising, put this on the team agenda and encourage everyone to discuss what is happening and what might be done about it. This on its own can make an important contribution to tackling the issue.

Be alert to stress symptoms in your subordinates. For example, someone who argues with you more than usual, or a person who is normally assertive but becomes unusually quiet, may be suffering from stress. As their manager you have a duty to take an interest. If you notice someone who does not normally smoke starting to do so, assume that it is a sign of stress. If someone is taking an excessive amount of sick leave, or their work suddenly deteriorates, this could be another indication.

Make time in your regular meetings with individuals and the team to talk about how people are feeling and whether they are experiencing undue stress. People may not readily admit it to you. They may talk instead about having too much work or excessively tight deadlines or lack of resources.

Your own actions may be an important cause of stress for others. If you are re-structuring, reducing the numbers employed or changing people's roles, you may lose sight of the impact it has on people. You can help those on the receiving end if you try to minimise uncertainty, clarify work objectives and redefine roles quickly. The list below suggests some strategies you might adopt.

Strategies for Minimising Stress during a Time of Change

STAFF DEVELOPMENT

- Help people reduce the stress they often place on themselves, by adopting realistic goals.
- Encourage people to adopt new goals that give alternative sources of satisfaction.
- Provide opportunities for in-service training designed to increase role effectiveness and adapt to change.
- Ensure that stress levels are monitored either in management supervision sessions or some other way.
- Offer work-focused counselling or consultation for those who are experiencing stress.
- Encourage the development of mutual support groups or networks.

JOBS AND ROLES

- Assist others to review their work load and priorities; where relevant consider how to reduce work loads, temporarily or permanently.
- Spread difficult or unrewarding work equitably.
- Increase opportunities at every level to exercise judgement, enhancing people's feelings of competence, ability to cope, and use of skills to make decisions.

- Structure roles and team arrangements to allow 'time out' sessons to occur.
- Consider using extra personnel to ease pressures during the transition phase of change.
- Insist that people take their holidays.
- Discourage frequent weekend and regular late-night working.
- Check to what extent people with subordinates are delegating.
- Clarify roles and responsibilities during a period of major change.
- Build career ladders.

MANAGEMENT DEVELOPMENT

- Develop training which focuses on current major problems.
- Monitor performance and give regular feedback.
- Watch for stress, intervene when strain is excessive.

ORGANISATIONAL MECHANISMS

- Do not change everything at once; leave a stable and secure base from which new arrangements can be explored.
- Give adequate time and resources to project teams and their leaders charged with implementing change.
- Create formal ways to encourage group and organisational problem solving.
- Promote involvement by maximising people's autonomy and participation in the change process.
- Formalise ways of handling conflict.
- Ensure adequate and direct feedback about new methods.
- Develop clear organisational goals and distinct values.

Try to be a model for other people in handling stress. When people see you refusing constantly to work excessively long hours, valuing your own personal time, making space for non-work activity, not being rushed, they realise that you are handling stress. They may soon find ways to do the same.

Further reading

LAZEAR J. *Meditations for Men Who Do Too Much.* Wellingborough, Aquarian Books, 1992

SCHAEF WILSON A. *Meditations for Women Who Do Too Much.* London, Harper & Row, 1990

17 *seventeen*

Time Management

John Spencer runs his own company, is a chartered accountant, is a world authority on UFOs, has written numerous books on management, is happily married and somehow also runs highly successful workshops on time management. Though he buzzes with ideas on how best to use time, what makes John so effective is his clear sense of purpose. He knows what he is trying to achieve, when he needs to complete his goals, and plans accordingly.

He is also excellent at handling paperwork. Despite his accountancy background he is a great 'chucker-away', keeping only what he is sure he will need. Like most people who are experts at personal goal and time management, John knows that there are three basic elements to managing your time well:

- people
- time
- paper

People

You have probably heard people claiming that time is money. They are wrong. It is far more accurate to say time is life. You can only make sense of using your time well when you know what you are trying to achieve – both at work and in the rest of your life.

Knowing broadly what your main life goals are, even writing them down, will help you manage your time well. Strangely, when you write down goals of any kind, they often have a curious habit of actually coming to pass.

To start using your time more effectively, try identifying what you want to achieve:

- in the next six months
- in the next two years
- in the next five years
- in the next 20 years.

No matter how insubstantial your thoughts may be, try to write something down. The very act of recording these ideas, no matter how vague they may at first appear, will contribute to making better sense of the day-to-day use of your time.

Do you know how much time there is available in which to achieve important work goals? Not as much as you may think. Most of us spend one third of our lives asleep, and one third away from work. Even if we work a heavy 10 or 12 hour day it is still not a lot for some people to achieve what they want. So using the time well really matters.

In the wider context of the organisation's future you will only tend to use time well and help others to do so when there is clarity about what the enterprise wants to be. The organisation's strategic intentions can fundamentally define how you and others actually spend your time.

There is evidence, for instance, that in most companies managers and leaders spend less than 3 per cent of their entire time really addressing the future of the organisation. Most of the time is devoted simply to running the business on a daily or monthly basis.

If you do free up time, therefore, it also matters what you do with it. If you merely invest it in more of the same activity, you are likely to get more of what you already have. As a manager who thinks strategically, therefore, you need to take a broad view of what your time is used for and where your energies are focused.

Time bandits

If someone entered your private space trying to steal your handbag or wallet, you would surely try to stop them. Yet at work we are often assailed by time bandits who take our precious time without our permission. They include useless phone calls, people insisting on conversations that get nowhere, quantities of paper demanding our attention, futile meetings and so on. What are your time bandits? See if you can devise a list of the worst offenders.

It requires a definite strategy to tackle the time bandits. Merely promising ourselves to be more efficient or to use our time well seldom works. Researchers estimate that one can increase personal productivity by as much as 20 per cent by improving personal time management. Nor is this merely a desirable result. If you are to avoid succumbing to stress at work, it pays to give real attention to time management (see also Chapter 16 on handling stress).

Time

Time management experts often tell people to keep a time log. In it you record and classify all the different actions you take, over several weeks. It is both hard work and incredibly boring, and most people stop long before they have enough reliable data to analyse.

You probably already know that you waste a fair amount of time, and you may even know why. It is doing something about it that can prove tricky. For the moment call your wasted time red time, and your efficiently used time green time. The whole point of good time management is learning to turn red time periods into green ones.

Red time can happen anywhere. It is also highly personal. For example, some people find staring out of the train window enjoyable, and consider it a worthwhile activity. Others regard it as wasting time. Seeing the boss or talking to an over-fussy supplier might be red time. What is *your* red time, and how much of it is there?

Converting red into green time is all about being more imaginative in how you allocate your time. For instance, by reading on the train you may turn potentially red time into green time. By discarding all those magazines not directly related to your immediate needs, you may gain some green time – you stop having occasional yet mainly useless forays into them scanning for something useful.

● Identify examples of your red time and see what imaginative ways you can find to convert it into green time.

When you are using your time as you want to use it, then it is undoubtedly green time. If you enjoy eating and do not see it as a waste of time, then make sure you really do enjoy it and do not rush the experience. Similarly, if you think watching television is mainly a waste of time, be sure to identify those few programmes that are worth watching and give yourself permission to sit and enjoy them.

The classic 80:20 rule usually applies to our use of time. We devote 20 per cent of our time to activity that is central to our aims, and 80 per cent on activity that is of marginal importance. We need to learn to do it the other way around, with 80 per cent of our time devoted to activity that we consider central to our aims.

Your body's time

Your body has its own version of red and green times. Research has shown that we each have a natural biorhythm, in which we are at our best only at certain times of our waking periods. Your body's green time is that period when you really function at your best. It might be first thing in the morning, a few hours around midday, or even around midnight. Knowing when you function at your best is an important way of improving your time management.

● Try to identify when you really function at your best – your body's internal green time.

This internal green time is usually only a few hours. So it pays to concentrate the most important things you have to do in that precious slot. For example, you might find that you make decisions more easily first thing in the morning and find it progressively harder as the day wears on. Good time management would therefore mean arranging to make as many important decisions as possible in the early part of the day.

Protect this precious time from attacks by time bandits. This could mean, for example, hanging a sign on your door asking not to be disturbed, finding a quiet place to work or arranging for a colleague to answer your phone during this time. Some people get the message across about their internal green time by putting a stuffed animal on their desk to signal that they must be left alone. In some companies with open plan office space, people put on coloured caps to warn that they are busy and do not want to be disturbed.

● Focus important tasks during your internal green time.
● Protect your internal green time from time bandits.

Paper

At the end of each day in the London Stock Exchange, every desk must be completely cleared. This is a security measure against possible bombs and terrorist activity. It means everyone must develop a way of dealing with the paper mountain they accumulate during the day. Some people dump everything in a cupboard or drawer. Others are more organised and ensure that all items are placed in files or particular drawers, where hopefully they can be found again.

In making decisions about each piece of paper that comes your way there are several useful guiding principles worth trying to apply. Even if you cannot follow them completely, they are powerful tools in helping you manage time well. The first two are:

- Take an overview first.
- Deal with each piece of paper once only.

The overview

You cannot make sense of the paperwork that comes your way if you keep dealing with each item in isolation. That way you are trying to hold all your priorities in your head and also ignoring the changing nature of the bombardment. Try to make a fixed time every day to review your paper work, rather than constantly trying to keep up with it as it changes. If you have only a few pieces of paper coming your way each day it may not matter if you deal with them as they arise, but if, like many busy managers, you have a considerable amount of correspondence to process, sticking to a definite time to deal with it is a useful discipline. It also uses your time more effectively.

The first step is to take an overview, in which you assess what each item requires. If you have an assistant or secretary your paperwork should reach you already sorted and labelled (see below). The overview also lets you prioritise the material so that you only tackle the important ones and let others handle the rest. Also, by prioritising them you ensure that if anything is neglected it is not the important items (see page 172).

Sort it

Try to ensure that papers arriving on your desk come in specific groups or folders:

- items for action, items addressed to you personally and non-routine communications
- material for signature
- reports, circulars, trade or professional information and material germane to your job
- background reading material such as journals or house magazines.

Dealing with each item once only

The ideal way of maximising your time in dealing with paper is only to process each item once, dealing with it when its turn comes and sending it on its way. In practice this may prove hard to achieve. You may find yourself hanging onto items in the expectation that you will read or deal with them later. The trouble with this approach is that these 'pending' items tend to build up and soon you are facing a depressing pile of items that you know need attention, but you cannot progress yet.

Even if you cannot always abide by this rule, you will find these other guidelines helpful:

- Dump it.
- Delegate it.
- Do it.
- Direct it.

Dump it On his travels Ulysses prevented his crew from hearing the fatal songs of the Sirens by stopping their ears with wax while he listened while lashed to the ship's mast. Have you heard the song of the *Storage Sirens*? The sounds they make are a similarly alluring trap of compelling tunes that can seriously distort your time management. For instance, one Storage Siren song repeats the hard to resist message: 'Someday, somebody may want this bit of paper – *save it, save it, save it.*'

Another is more threatening. It goes: 'If you throw this piece of paper away you may bitterly regret it, for heavens sake – *save it, save it, save it.*'

One of the more subtle songs is all about *how* you save your papers. You may be tempted to have a simple, understandable system, but the Storage Sirens tempt you with an irresistible song that goes: 'Create a complete system – *expand it, expand it, expand it.*'

Like Ulysses, part of you will undoubtedly want to obey the Sirens, because the sounds are so compelling. They make such sweet sense, why risk problems by ignoring their commands?

Resisting them is essential for taking charge of your own time. Nowadays the Sirens are crooning not just about paper and paper storage systems but about electronic ones too. Their power is demonstrated on millions of computers that are cluttered with countless files of dead data. Yet no one ever has the time to clear out this dead material.

The success of the Storage Sirens explains why even quite small companies possess filing cabinets packed with dead paper. Most of it conforms strictly to the 80:20 rule, that is, 80 per cent of the work done by the organisation is handled by around 20 per cent of the papers on file.

If you obey the Storage Sirens, paper accumulates in frightening quantities. Soon it begins to choke up desks and floors. Worst of all, large amounts are left lying around in full view, making you feel pressured and less efficient.

How can you counter the effects of the Storage Sirens? The first step is to take a personal interest in your own filing system, insisting that it remains as simple as possible. The more elaborate the structure, the harder it may be to maintain or to keep under control. If you cannot quickly check through the entire contents in a few hours it is probably not serving you well. A simple structure means you or your assistant will be able to rapidly:

- find your way around it
- weed out dead material.

Some managers regard half a dozen bulging filing cabinets in or just outside their office as a sort of virility symbol. For others it is a kind of security blanket. It suggests that they are busy, important people. Yet these same systems can seriously impinge on their personal efficiency and use of time, not just because items are hard to find, but because they are a burden to maintain and make everyone feel weighed down.

Delegate it An important contribution to using your time more productively is to pass unwanted paper to someone else. Much of the material coming your way is either nothing much to do with you, or requires only a brief response.

Rather than preparing an elaborate memo to send the thing on its way, just write a note on the original material indicating your response or saying that you regard the item as one for the other person's attention rather than yours. Put each item through a simple filter by asking: 'Can someone else deal with this apart from me?' This will force you to consider how you can pass work on to others, enlarging their jobs at the same time.

Do it Some papers do require action. These are the ones that you really want to identify from the mass of material that may well flow across your desk. Apply the *urgency/importance* guide to deciding what precise action is required (see page 172).

Papers that require action can, of course, always be put back in your tray for action later. This is fine if you only have a few such items, but if you have dozens of them, the mounting pile begins to have an adverse effect on your time management. The investigation of the much publicised near disaster at the Three Mile Island nuclear plant in America reviewed the company's filing system. Amongst the many papers were ones predicting the crisis and demanding action. Somehow the managers concerned had either not got round to reading them or not taken action.

Every business has the equivalent of a Three Mile Island incident waiting to happen. You could have one lurking somewhere in your life. Good time management means handling all the papers that reach you appropriately and expeditiously. You can only do that if you are properly organised.

Tips for handling paper:

- Make a decision.

- Do not let the paper stand still for long; it is much harder to deal with once it turns into a pile.

- Know how to find what you file, which means regularly clearing obsolete files.

- Minimise repeat contact – try to process each piece of paper only once or at most twice.

- For papers in a pile, work one day from the top downwards, and the next day work from the bottom upwards.

- Avoid pending trays with papers hanging around for attention, with no set date for processing.

- Consign current papers that you are not working on at this moment to a 'bring forward' file divided into useful time periods such as daily, weekly or monthly sections.

Direct it to filing   The place for paper you do not currently need is in storage containers such as filing cabinets or computer-based systems that convert paper materials for electronic storage. Keep only a few essential files in your own desk or personal filing cabinet – highly confidential ones and those you are working on currently. You should know what they are and expect to use them regularly.

Direct all other papers to either a central filing system or an archive facility.

Sorting

A useful tip is to divide your incoming material into three broad categories such as A, B and C items.

- A items are ones that *must* be done, no matter what happens; they are simply inescapable.
- B items are ones you should *probably* deal with but you are not yet certain.
- C items are things that might be nice to do.

Put all C items into a drawer. Ignore this material until you are forced to dig into the drawer and relocate something.

This 'C drawer' has a useful habit of seldom demanding attention. Most of the items will die a natural death and you can dump them permanently after a few days or weeks. But beware: the C drawer can make you feel more secure about not throwing things away prematurely but it only really works well if you regularly weed out the contents.

Many of the ideas for dealing effectively with paper apply just as much to E-mail systems, where people communicate to each other via computer. E-mail systems make it easy to circulate information to a host of other people. Those on the receiving end can soon find they are spending inordinate amounts of time simply reading the messages to learn which are significant.

Simple sort methods, such as scanning for key names, current topics and other trigger devices may help to winnow out material. For example, Bill Gates of Microsoft has his E-mail system filter out all messages from people he does not know personally.

Lists

Many successful people, especially in business, maintain constantly renewed lists of things they want to do. Do you have an action list? If not, now is the time to create one. However, lists can dominate your life if you are not careful. They can become a burden rather than a help unless you organise them properly.

The two kinds of lists to consider are:

● the master list
● the daily 'to do' list.

The master list

First, try writing down absolutely everything you think you need to do at work. Avoid being too general, such as writing down your entire job description. Be specific – list as many tasks or activities that you know demand your current attention. Do not worry about how long the list stretches. It may run to two, three or even more pages. If you prefer, create the list on a computer screen. This potentially large list is called your *master* list.

Master lists can be daunting and are often wrongly used as a regular daily guide to action. Their real value is as a source of guidance about the broad range of activities you must pursue. To prevent the master list ruling your life, use it only as a reference source for deciding what will go on your '*to do*' list for the day.

The daily 'to do' list

Your list of things to do each day can never be very long. There are simply not enough hours available for a long list, no matter how hard you work. Moreover the nature of most managerial work is that you are responding to unexpected situations, so the daily 'to do' list is not always achievable. Identifying those things you *really* intend to achieve today requires thought and a ruthless sense of reality. You can only achieve so much, and often less than you think. So your list is unlikely to have more than 10 items on it.

Any items on your daily 'to do' list which are not completed that day should go on the next day's list. Items that keep being moved back to the following day are ones you do not really want to tackle or are proving to have a low priority, or both. Items appearing more than three times on the daily 'to do' list, should be:

- dropped entirely
- allocated serious time
- delegated.

Prioritising

Lists are a helpful way of capturing how you might spend your time. They usually need refining, however, otherwise they tend to get ever longer. If items are not removed, they start to harm your time management rather than help it. A principle that has stood the test of time is the *urgency/importance* criterion. This judges your potential activities in terms of how far they are urgent and important.

Items which are both urgent and important should normally be done by you, while those that are important but not necessarily urgent might be passed on to others, so enlarging their jobs.

Similarly, items that have a high urgency rating but are not extremely important are also good candidates for passing on. See the chart below.

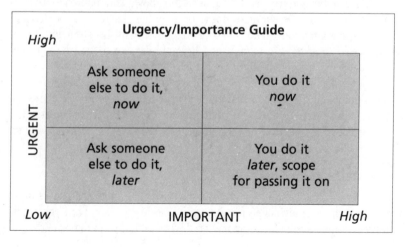

More time management tips:

- Write memos on the received item and send it back.
- Dial your own calls, it is generally quicker.
- Ensure that phone messages are on proper message pads and message takers are trained.
- Pass on authority for tasks as much as possible – wait for people to tell you that they are overloaded.
- If you spend more than 10 per cent of your total work time travelling, rethink your working methods.
- Explain to people that when your door is open you welcome callers; when it is shut you must only be disturbed in an emergency.
- If you need to meet a deadline, take time away from the office to work in a quiet place.
- Ask for all reports to start with a one page summary.
- Do not personally chase progress, except as a last resort.

You will find it a fascinating and rewarding exercise to invite colleagues to share with you the ways in which they maximise their own time. What tricks and techniques do they use that seem to work for them? Why, for example, do some people swear by neatly-folding leather organisers while others rely on a spiral bound day book in which to record everything they must do?

Further reading

GODEFROY, C. H. AND CLARK J. *The Complete Time Management System.* London, Piatkus, 1989

LAKEIN A. *How to Get Control of Your Time and Your Life.* London, Signet, 1973

18 *eighteen*

Listening

Most managers are good talkers. They need strong verbal skills both to communicate what they want and to persuade. The more successful the manager, the better they tend to be at communicating. Yet while we wholly think of communication in terms of speaking, it is also about listening.

Some companies have attached so much importance to listening that they have even defined themselves in those terms. In the USA Sperry Rand defined the company image as 'we listen', while the Midland Bank called itself the Listening Bank.

Listening is not merely staying silent. For managers there are several sorts of listening. You can do it to:

● monitor the environment

● take in someone's messages

● promote communication.

Monitoring the environment

This is a macro-activity compared to listening to what any one person may be saying. When monitoring the environment you are alert, taking in signals, absorbing information, hearing messages about the big picture. This 'big picture' is not the individual, it is the climate in which your organisation is currently operating. It is also the one that has not yet arrived. When you are listening strategically, you are alert to any input that could determine how the organisation achieves its strategic intentions. It means being hungry for information that will help the organisation transform itself.

For example, when you hear on the morning radio as you are preparing to leave for work that some change has occurred that could affect your business, this is building the big picture. When you attend a conference and someone talks about a new technological development that could radically alter some aspect of how your organisation functions, that too is adding to the big picture.

Listening so as to build the big picture is an essential skill. Gradually you will learn to filter out all sorts of irrelevant sounds and messages. Some of this filtering is entirely unconscious. You do it naturally without even planning it. However, there is also active listening to identify the information that can sharpen or alter the big picture. To do this you have to have a sense of what you are listening for and why.

Active listening to enhance the big picture is easier when you have a sense of your current priorities, when you know what your organisation, division or section is trying to achieve. You can then listen in the correct frame of mind. Within your organisation you might listen in order to discover:

● what customers you are now serving

● through what channels customers are reaching you

● who your competitors are today

● what the basis of your current competitive advantage is

● what skills or capabilities make you unique today.

You actively listen to people talking about what is happening so as to answer these questions. While you may already know the answers, the chances are that they are already starting to change.

In listening to build the big picture of the future, you might try to discover:

● what customers you will be serving in the future

● through what channels you will reach your customers in the future

● who your competitors will be in the future

● what skills or capabilities will make you unique in the future.

These help you to think strategically.

Taking in someone's messages

To get things done as a manager you depend on influencing others. This means being able to make conversations work for rather than against you. What you say and how you say it, how you listen and convey that you are doing so, will partly determine your ability to produce results through others.

You do not control conversations, although with practice your can certainly control your side of them. In gaining this control you automatically begin to influence other people and their response to what you want.

Conversation skills include handling personal criticism, making proposals, registering a protest, disagreeing without aggression, responding creatively, negotiating, and so on. Some of these, such as acting assertively or negotiating are dealt with in other chapters.

You are skilled at handling conversations if you:

- listen in a positive way at the right time
- talk meaningfully when it is your turn
- know how to alter the direction of the conversation acceptably
- can keep the communication moving at a comfortable pace
- build on key points the other party raises
- deal with differences of opinion
- find out what people think
- provide positive feedback
- have the right word for the right occasion.

We spend 80 per cent of our waking lives communicating in some way and the biggest slice (40 per cent) is devoted to listening. Despite this, few people receive training in it. Managers who have discovered the power of listening, for instance, have mainly done so through trial and error. But many organisations now recognise the importance of learning to listen, and some even train their employees so that they can do it better.

Colleagues and subordinates should ideally see you as someone who understands them and is sensitive to their feelings and what they say. Those who report directly to you expect you to be genuinely interested in helping them perform well. You can do that partly by demonstrating that you take in their messages and respect what they say.

Selective hearing

Research has confirmed that we all tend to hear what we want to hear. For example, if a piece of information makes us feel uncomfortable or is not to our liking, we will endeavour to avoid really absorbing it.

Selective hearing explains why managers may consistently ignore information that might otherwise help them avoid important mistakes. Thus a manager may ignore someone's pleas that they are overworked until eventually the person solves the problem by becoming sick or leaving.

Sexual and other kinds of discrimination are other examples where managers may find it so uncomfortable to deal with the implications that they screen out the information and eventually just ignore it. Many cases have come before the courts where it has been shown that managers were told more than once about a sexual harassment issue yet chose to believe that it was somehow unreal.

Financial crises are one of the most significant reasons why organisations are forced to make major changes in direction or policy. Yet often the financial facts have been presented in oral form many times, apart from also being put in writing. Anxious finance directors have often tried many times to explain their concerns but their audience while apparently listening, never seemed to take it in until too late.

When you take the trouble to really listen to other people's messages you:

- discover what is happening and the nature of current problems
- learn how problems have altered
- learn how to deal with people, how their minds work and how they approach problems
- access a rich source of ideas for improvements
- convey the message: 'I care'
- gain clues as to how to avoid future problems
- give people a chance to express their feelings about their jobs
- increase the chances that other people will listen to you.

Listening to other people's messages is easy to learn but hard to turn into a habit. The only realistic answer is constant practice. For example, when you are engaged in a conversation with someone, do you tend to wait for your turn to speak? By doing that you are not devoting your full attention to listening. People soon realise that you are listening merely so as to know when you can speak next.

We do not just listen so as to know when it is out turn to speak. We also do it to:

- understand
- remember
- recall.

When we listen to understand we are trying to become more aware of what is going on, what the other person really means. Thus there are two powerful listening questions you can ask yourself while you are not speaking:

- What does this person really *mean* by what they are saying?
- How does this person *feel* right now?

If you do nothing else while listening, if you try to answer these questions your listening will certainly improve. These apparently simple questions can help you look beyond just the words to uncover the true message.

The average person talks to you at around 125 words a minute. Yet you think at up to 500 words a minute. Why not use this spare capacity fully? Most of the time, instead of active listening we become distracted, pass superficial and rapid judgements, or silently concentrate on preparing our own response. If we are to remember what someone is saying we cannot just sit there passively hoping it will all be absorbed for future use. We need to listen hard for words and phrases that will tend to fix the information in our minds.

Similarly we may later want to recall what someone has said. We can help our recall by making associations between their messages and something that will make it easy to bring the information to mind later. For example, if someone tells you that their department has increased its output by 31 per cent, you may not easily recall this precise percentage. However, by imagining them standing by a giant apple that is cut into thirds, you may implant the fact indelibly in your mind until you later need to recall it.

Bad listening habits:

- branding the subject as uninteresting
- criticising a speaker's delivery or mannerisms
- getting too stimulated by what the speaker says
- listening only for facts
- faking attention
- becoming distracted
- avoiding difficult material
- allowing emotion-laden words to arouse personal antagonism, daydreaming and wasting the benefits of thought speed.

You can enhance your listening by allowing adequate time to hear. When you are rushed or you force someone else to hurry with their communication, you immediately reduce your chances of hearing well.

When people describe their contacts with really successful managers they often say things like, 'He always seems to have time for me', or 'When she listens to me I feel as if I'm the most important person in the world for her at that moment.' There is no magic in gaining that kind of reputation. It is simply a case of taking the listening role extremely seriously. For instance, encourage people to take their time talking to you. Show by your words and actions that you are ready to devote your whole attention to them. Similarly, try always to let them terminate the conversation rather than doing so yourself.

Another step you can take is to eliminate interruptions. If you are constantly answering the phone, dealing with people popping their head around your door, signing letters and so on, the message you are giving is unmistakeable. You are busy and have not really got the time for the person and their message.

Other factors that can make it harder for you to be a good listener include excessive background noise, such as people tapping on keyboards or making phone calls. Likewise bad lighting and papers all over your desk can indicate to the other person that speaking to you is not going to be an easy experience. The simple expedient of visibly clearing up the papers on your desk while indicating to the person that you are ready to hear them can show that you really are a listener.

Energy

Active listening means showing with your whole body that you are focused on the other person. You need to expend energy doing this, paying attention to where you put your hands, how you hold your body, the way you walk from one place to another.

Good listening means staying awake both mentally and physically. You may find difficulty with these if you are over-tired. So having enough sleep and staying fresh is an important part of being an effective listener. Even small signs can signal to the other person that you are not really paying attention. For example, if you are over-tired you may try to disguise the fact by holding holding your body upright, but your eyes may give you away by gradually closing or taking a long time to complete each blink.

Promoting communication

Three other essentials for enhancing your listening capabilities are:

● attending
● making requests
● expressing understanding.

Attending

Use non-verbal methods to help show that you are giving the other person the attention they deserve. Attending behaviour includes:

- *Making eye contact.* Hold it for at least 70–80 per cent of the time. More than this may make the other person feel uncomfortable. When breaking contact, avoid looking all over the place or darting your eyes from side to side.

- *Using body language.* Position your body towards the other person, and nod regularly to show that you either agree or are paying attention. Use facial muscles to express interest and other emotions. Assume a relaxed, not a slouched position. Avoid folded arms as this places a barrier between you and the other person. For very intense listening try leaning forward, elbows on the table with your chin resting on your hands while looking at the other person. Mirroring the body position of the other person is another way of signalling that you are listening to what they are saying. For example, if the other person crosses their legs, you might do the same; if they place their hands in a steeple shape you might do so too.

Making requests

A sign that you are listening is that you can ask relevant questions, seek additional information or request clarification about something they have said.

Ask open-ended questions as part of your listening strategy. These encourage the other person to continue talking, and to do so covering a wide territory. They cannot be answered by a straight yes or no and require the other person to expand, think and elaborate. Use expressions like:

- I'd like to hear how things went while I was away.
- Tell me about . . .
- What do you feel about . . .
- That is interesting, can you elaborate a bit further?

Try posing fact-seeking questions. These ask the person to provide information while also showing that you have heard what they have said so far. Use these questions in an encouraging way, rather than posing them as if your are conducting an interrogation.

Probing is a way of showing that you are listening by encouraging the person to become more specific. Do so in a patient manner that is fairly neutral. For example:

- In what way do you feel that pressures on the team are increasing?
- Can you give me an example?
- Tell me how I could do what you suggest?
- Would you like to explain how best I can help?

Give encouragement through verbal signals that you are interested to hear more. Use short words or phrases such as 'mmmm', 'uh huh', 'I see' or 'really?', accompanied by a nod of your head.

Other non-verbal messages that show that you are listening include nodding, eyebrow raising, quizzical but interested looks, leaning forward and smiling. The importance of these signs cannot be overestimated. When you fail to use them people will quite often rapidly grind to a halt in their speaking.

Expressing understanding

When you convey to someone that you have been listening you help reduce the inevitable communication gaps that exist between people. You can do this by:

- reflecting back feelings
- paraphrasing
- summarising.

It is sometimes more important to respond to the way someone is feeling than to their actual words. For instance, someone may be saying something in a calm way yet clearly be bubbling over with an emotion, such as enthusiasm, anxiety or anger. When listening, try to detect the underlying emotion that the words may not be conveying. If you consider that the feelings are more important than the words, demonstrate your ability to truly 'hear' what is being said by reflecting back with expressions like:

- It seems you are feeling . . .
- It sounds to me as if . . .
- You must be really . . . (angry, pleased, worried etc.)

Another clear sign that you are listening well is being able to repeat back to the person what they have said in your own words. Paraphrase the content of their communication, not their emotions.

Paraphrasing also allows the other person to correct misunderstandings and shows you are listening with care. Key word repetition is another form of paraphrasing. When you are really listening it is easy to pick out particular words or phrases to encourage the speaker to explain in more detail.

Similarly, if a speaker is developing a theme you can help them by adding constructively to what they have said. Examples of the kind of questions that promote extensions include:

- How do you mean?
- What makes you say that?
- What are you thinking of specifically?
- Tell me more.

When you summarise what someone has said you again convey the extent of your active listening. You condense the information into brief points or themes and focus rambling remarks into crisp phrases. Like paraphrasing, this technique demonstrates that you are taking in what the person is saying.

You might introduce the paraphrase or summary with something like:

- As I understand it . . .
- If I've got it right . . .
- So what you are saying is . . .'

Listening in a group

Much of your daily listening will probably occur in a group, such as a team, a meeting, a conference, a sales presentation. In these situations it is only too easy to switch off either permanently or temporarily and hardly absorb anything of value.

To ward of the tendency to doze, to listen too selectively or simply to lose concentration, you need to listen with specific aims in mind. These force you to concentrate on some mental gymnastics. They make your mind do the equivalent of press-ups or running on the spot.

Techniques for listening in a group:

- Check what new ideas, goals, or solutions seem to be emerging. Can you write them down in order of importance?
- Identify what facts need further clarifying, and how.
- Specify the missing information.
- Identify what opinions, judgements, values or convictions come to mind.
- Try developing an idea already expressed by someone else; explain it, elaborate it, analyse it. Find some examples, illustrations or explanations.

- Find the relationship between the various facts you are hearing. Can you integrate these into a single theme, argument or point?
- Analyse what might prod the group to greater activity, such as reminding it of the importance of the task, its limited resources or its deadlines.
- Keep your own set of written records to serve as the group memory.
- Watch to see whom you should encourage to speak next.
- Identify who is talking too much and find a way to reduce this behaviour. Who is dominating the conversation or preventing others from speaking openly?

Listening techniques keep you listening actively, rather than passively letting the sounds flow over you. For example, if you attend a conference or a large meeting it is only too easy to sit back and allow speaker after speaker to talk, without ever fully paying attention.

Try disciplining yourself to either take notes of the main points being made, or better still start drawing a mind map. Mind maps can keep you awake, even alert during the most boring situations since creating them is itself a challenge. You can become so involved with drawing the map that the time simply flashes by. But use note taking judiciously and avoid note mania. You do not, for example, demonstrate that you are listening to someone if you are tapping your notes into a lap-top computer. Writing too much while listening may also inadvertently convey the message, 'I'm recording this for the record, so watch what you are saying.'

When you listen using the kind of techniques listed above they both help your concentration and counteract any tendency to interrupt. When you do finally speak, your impact is that much greater.

Further reading

MARGERISON C. *Conversation Control Skills for Managers*. London, Mercury Books, 1987

19 *nineteen*

Better Reading

Reading is an obsession with many top people. By demanding and then processing large amounts of information they gain immense knowledge and an ability to ask penetrating questions. Managers often complain about the amount of reading matter they must process. Computers and E-mail have made this problem worse. It is so easy to distribute multiple copies around the network that large numbers of useless messages accumulate, demanding attention.

One of the legendary management readers was Harold S. Geneen, the head of International Telegraph and Telephone. Over two decades his grasp of detail was dreaded by subordinates. Each month he absorbed all the progress reports sent to him, which filled a book 10 inches thick. He regularly went home carrying three bulging cases filled with papers, arriving back early next day having read them all. The newspaper proprietor, Lord Thomson, read company reports as if they were cheap novels. He whizzed through them at an enormous rate last thing at night, before he went to sleep.

Reading fast is essential to being a successful manager, because of the continued increase in the amount of written or visual material bombarding us. Apart from hard copy in the form of memos, reports, letters, magazines, sales literature and so on, we are also facing an enormous upsurge in electronic material to read. Many companies could now hardly survive without their E-mail systems, yet these can generate huge quantities of items to sift and discard.

What is all this reading for? Much of it will be merely so that you can manage day-to-day matters. But if you are not careful you will soon be overloaded with vast amounts of information that is mainly concerned with the past – reports, memos, correspondence, surveys and so on.

In the wider context of the organisation's strategic intentions, your reading needs to be partly directed towards the future. Reading in order to understand and make sense of the future is a leadership rather than a managerial activity. It will tend to set you apart from managers who lose sight of what their job is really about.

In reading so as to manage the future, you will constantly be relating material to core strategic issues such as whether the information will help you enter new markets, whether it will help you understand who your future competitors will be, what it tells you about your future customers and how to reach them.

Even if you are brilliant at handling reading matter, however, managing people well is more likely to help you succeed in the long term. Faced with the choice of people versus paper, many managers rightly choose the former. Paper can nearly always wait.

You are nevertheless unlikely to escape the daily round of reading that accompanies most managerial roles. Treating the reading task as low priority is usually a mistake since it allows you to absorb far more information than you can through oral means and at your own pace. You, rather than someone speaking, control the communication process.

Developing reading skills

You may feel that you already read quite adequately, and in the purely technical sense that is probably true. There may be room for improvement, however, in the way you do it. You need to develop your reading skills if you:

- always start at the beginning of text and diligently read through everything to the end
- sub-vocalise, including moving your lips even slightly when reading
- read at less than 350 words a minute
- have difficulty in scanning quickly and obtaining salient points
- have poor recall and comprehension
- tend to reread words or sentences you have just read
- feel impatient, bored or unable to concentrate when reading
- often puzzle over the meaning of words
- feel pressured, with insufficient time for reading
- have difficulty coping with incoming paper work.

Effective managers develop sound reading habits to enhance their personal impact. This means that you need a reading strategy, a personal plan of action for handling the reading task. It is likely to cover two key abilities:

- searching for salient items essential for doing your job well
- quickly processing large amounts of information.

Searching

If you were given a book with your name printed somewhere in the text and told to find it in three minutes you could almost certainly do so. You would probably scan the pages fast, just hunting for that familiar shape of your name. You would easily ignore all other material.

When we are reading with a definite purpose ,we can cover an enormous amount of material quickly. It is possible, for example, to skim successfully through a complete book of 60,000 words in a minute or less when you know exactly what you are seeking.

If we know clearly what we want, we direct our brain to exclude irrelevant material and focus only on what we are seeking. Searching under these circumstances is almost an unconscious activity; you just trust your brain and eyes to do the work.

One of the most powerful means of speeding up your reading is therefore to develop greater clarity about the purpose behind each reading task. Try to approach the material by asking yourself what information you are seeking.

The search for information is different from allowing yourself to wander around the text in a leisurely way, savouring writing style or contents. It is a hunt against time and is results-based.

While speed is important, however, it need not be the entire focus of your reading development. You also need to read better, for example, by organising your reading material so that it best suits your needs. This may mean sorting out reading material first, before even attempting to tackle it. Thus you might create a pile to which you consign all trade journals and other magazines, and rather than reading them in bits and pieces during the day, you would set yourself a definite time slot to deal with them. Moreover, if you can switch to relying on an abstracts service for much of your professional reading you will cover a wide range of issues and only read the full items of material that you feel are more important.

You can also protect yourself from many wasteful reading habits by organising how material reaches you. For instance, how much preliminary sorting of material can you have done on your behalf? You may be able to get someone else to cover certain publications and incoming material for you, so that you only receive relevant items, or ones for decision. Similarly, you could insist, as IBM managers once did, that no memorandum should be longer than one page. When you ask someone for a report, you can insist that unless it is only a couple of pages long, it must always be supplied with a one-page management summary.

External factors

Apart from what happens inside your head, there are some important external factors to consider in improving your reading. The first is your environment. You cannot expect to read well in a hot, stuffy room with lots of noise, or when you are cold. It is surprising how often managers attempt serious reading when the environment is working against them. If you are doing anything other than gentle leisure reading, make sure the environment is comfortable and supports you when concentrating.

It may be tempting to slump in your chair when reading and this too can militate against reading well. For example, if you read a book or a report while looking downwards at it on your lap, your eyes are more likely to start to close than if you have the material and yourself fully upright.

Speed

Most people believe that they read faster than in fact they do. Check your present reading speed right now. It is easy to do and will give you a base line for reading the rest of this chapter.

Check your present reading speed

- Count the number of words on three pages of a book (choose a relatively easy one). A quick way is to count the number of words in several lines and use the average, multiplied by the number of pages.

- Time how long it takes to read three pages of the book.

- Divide the number of words by the number of minutes it takes to read them.

- The formula is:

$$\text{Words read per minute} = \frac{\text{Number of pages read} \times \text{number of words per page}}{\text{Number of minutes spent reading the words}}$$

You can almost certainly handle more reading than your currently do. Even if you increased your present weekly bombardment of material by 20 or 30 times, you would still have plenty of spare mental capacity. Your brain can handle vast amounts of extra information. Like a computer it has impressive powers to make connections between different facts or ideas. Its ability to see links between apparently disparate facts and knowledge is awesome.

We tend to think of reading as merely understanding what the author intended. It is far more than that. A manager who reads well can:

- assimilate the information
- integrate it with existing knowledge and experience
- retain it for later use
- recall it when needed
- communicate.

Reading technique How do you read? Use your forefinger to trace what you believe to be the movement and the speed of your eyes. Most people asked to do this will trace a smooth path from left to right, with a quick jump from the end of one line to the beginning of the next. This zig-zagging movement is usually shown as taking between a quarter to one second for each line.

In fact this seriously underestimates what happens with even the slowest reader. Even if your eye moved at only one line per second, you would still cover over 600 words per minute. Since the average for people's actual reading speed for even easy material is only around 250 words per minute, our eyes clearly cover the words far more quickly than we realise.

Eye Movements

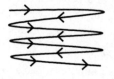

How most people think the eye moves when reading text

 *words*

How the eye actually moves.
Eyes jump in a stop/start way

 *words*

Eye movements of a faster reader; more words are read in each jump, with no skipping back

Rather than moving in smooth lines, our eyes really move in a series of short, quick jumps and stops, as the chart on page 188 shows. While these jumps take almost no time, the pauses can take from a quarter to one and half seconds. If you are a slow reader you will tend to read one word at a time, skipping back over words and letters. Your stops will also tend to be longer. The result is a much slower reading speed than you are capable of achieving.

Speeding up your reading is therefore mainly about expanding the number of words read during each eye jump. The more efficient you are as a reader, the more words you can cover with each eye movement jump. For example, really slow readers cover only one or two words in a single eye jump. Slightly faster readers may cover four or five words at a time. Still faster ones may be able to take in a whole line in one jump, without skipping back. Super-fast readers have learned how to make their eyes make big jumps rights across an entire line. Eventually they can run their eyes rapidly down the centre of a page and still understand what they are reading.

Slower readers therefore do more work. Making smaller jumps makes it harder to comprehend material. Faster, smoother readers gain the meaning of the text and thus do not need to understand and note every word. You simply do less work as a quicker reader because your eyes are stopping and starting less per page.

Some fast-reading facts

- Your present average reading speed is not necessarily ideal; you may simply not be using the best reading strategy.

- You can easily learn to read more than 500 words per minute; with practice you may be able to reach 1000 words or more.

- Even when you read fast you can still expect to understand material, since you are concentrating on it more and have more time to return to areas of special interest.

- The faster you go, the more impetus you gather and the more you tend to concentrate.

Most reading is done at a relaxed, almost lazy pace. This means that there is ample scope for speeding up, while still maintaining or even improving comprehension and retention. Schools seldom do much more than teach you to recognise words and sentences. Few people are trained to understand how the eye traverses the page or the techniques for reading material, sifting, recall, note taking, concentration, handling boredom and so on.

The result is that many managers are not only slow readers, they do not even enjoy it. Since you are reading this part of the book, you are at least sufficiently interested to want to do it better. Motivation is a critical success factor in most learning but particularly so with faster reading.

Improving your reading speed Speed-reading classes can certainly raise your reading speed, often to impressive levels. But it is frequently only a temporary gain. You can usually do just as well without a course and by practising at home. Speed courses merely use your new motivation to read better. Because you want to improve, you do. After the course, however, the discipline it imposes ends and seldom permanently alters your whole approach.

The Metronome

Use a metronome to help you increase your reading speed.

Set it ticking at a reasonable pace, with each beat indicating a single sweep of your eyes. This helps to acquire a smooth, steady rhythm. It counteracts the natural tendency to slow down after a while.

Once you have found a comfortable rhythm, you can increase your reading speed by gradually adding an extra beat per minute.

Use the machine to pace yourself so that eventually each beat represents one page you are sweeping.

A purely mechanical aid you can adopt is a metronome, normally used for keeping musical rhythm (see above). Other exercises include:

- Use a card to cover all but one line of a page – read this line with one sweep of the eyes, then move the card to reveal the next line. Gradually increase the speed with which the card moves down the page.

- Read as fast as you can for one minute without bothering about comprehension.

- Practise turning 100 pages at roughly two seconds for each page, moving the eyes very rapidly down the page; do this in short sessions of about two minutes.

- Ask a friend to select a paragraph or sentence from a book without you seeing which part it comes from. Then try to find the chosen text, giving yourself first five minutes, then four minutes and so on. Now try the same approach with the main idea behind an article.

- Select some paragraphs from a long piece of text that seem to stand out from the rest. Scan through, looking for themes and major lines of arguments. You can extend this further by taking a business article and deliberately only reading the first sentence of each paragraph and perhaps the last one. See how much you can absorb of the whole text from just this sampling.

- Try reading a whole book in two minutes! Turn the pages as fast as you can, taking in as many words as possible without stopping. Force yourself to race through the material. When you return to ordinary reading you will find your average reading speed is now higher, perhaps twice as fast as before.

One blockage you may face is anxiety. You may worry about whether you will find what you want, understand the material or remember it. You may also be concerned about whether you really can improve your reading ability. Yet in reading better you do not really do anything very different; you just do it more efficiently. It comes mainly from practice and motivation. So one device is to give yourself a series of rewards for completing reading tasks such as speed exercises.

Skimming

Skimming involves going through reading material incredible fast, not bothering to take in everything. Instead you read highly selectively, looking for certain signs that it is time to slow down and pay more attention to the content.

Experienced managers can skim vast quantitites of information in minutes and still find the salient points. For example, review the contents of a business magazine, or a report on your desk. Look at the contents list, the titles, the subheadings, the illustrations, words in italics, in fact anything that stands out from the mass of words. Try to find the pattern or structure of the material before plunging into it.

Similarly, concentrate your attention on nouns and verbs rather than adjectives or prepositions.

Memory

The assumption most people make is that the faster they read the less they will retain. Speed, however is not the most decisive factor in governing what you recall. Remembering what you read is based on several factors:

- putting the material into a frame of reference
- understanding
- strong memory traces
- reinforcement.

Context

As a manager you will read a wide variety of material, whether in paper or electronic form. The wider the range of material the harder it may be to make sense of it initially. You may, for example, be halfway through the second page of a report before you grasp the context in which it is written.

Memorising depends initially on being able to put the reading matter in some form of recognisable context. This context helps you begin to classify and analyse the material. Right from the start, therefore, you should be looking to establish the context. In which 'box' does it fit, where should you place it within the whole range of your managerial responsibilities? Once you are clear on the context you will more readily remember the contents.

Understanding

Naturally, knowing the context is not much use unless you also understand the material. Much that is written for managers, both within an organisation and from outside it, is unnecessarily complicated and lacking in brevity. You may not have much control over how people outside the organisation write, but you will certainly be able to influence what is sent to you from within it.

For example, you can insist on material being presented in summary form, and in short paragraphs and sentences. You can wage a war against jargon, since even when you know what it means it can still slow your comprehension.

When you understand material without having to translate it or work out what complex phraseology means, your chances of remembering the salient points are much increased.

Memory traces

An important factor in memorising material is the strength of the memory trace attached to the information. The trace lets you recall the material because your mind can literally 'find' what it is you are seeking. For a trace to have strength you rely on:

- association
- motivation.

You tend to remember something you have read when it is also strongly associated with a memorable picture, idea, pattern, arrangement, event and so on. So, for example, you may have trouble remembering a complicated telephone number as a straightforward sequence of numbers:

0488717588

However by rearranging it into a different pattern it may be easier to memorise:

04 88 71 75 88

Alternatively, an item of information may be made more memorable because it is associated with something that is not easily forgotten. For instance, in one report to a senior mangement group a manager described the danger of something going wrong as the 'Humpty Dumpty Effect'. People tended to remember the material associated with it because of the memorable association.

Reinforcement

You cannot assume that one reading alone will commit a piece of material to memory. You may need to reinforce your recollection in various ways until the information 'sticks'.

In the early stages of memorising something you may rapidly forget material unless it is reinforced in some way. You may need to return to it at quite short intervals initially to strengthen the memory. Gradually, however, the gaps between the different renforcements reduce until the memory becomes permanent.

There will be vast amounts of material that you do not need to memorise at all, so that reinforcement is not necessary. However, when you have identified the information you want to remember, you can improve your chances of being able to recall it later if you consciously set out to reinforce it several times.

Further reading

WRIGHT C. (ed.) *Communication Skills*. (Chapter Five.) London, Industrial Society, 1993

20 *twenty*

Assertiveness

You are in a meeting with some important people and want to make a point. Every time you start to speak someone gets in first. Finally you get a word in, only to be stopped in your tracks by someone who rises saying that they have to leave. Their departure is the cue for everyone else to depart. Before you know it, the meeting is over. Furious, you walk back to your office wondering how it happened. How was it that you never really made your presence felt? Why did you never manage to get your point across, especially as it was a good one?

While you are ruminating on these events the person chairing the meeting catches up with you. She says that she missed hearing your comments and wondered if there was anything you wanted to say. You are still so annoyed with yourself for not speaking up that you tell her that if the meeting had been managed better you would have been asked for your views. Still angry, you continue on your way.

Not speaking up during a meeting is an example of being unassertive, while being angry with the chairperson and putting her down is an example of aggression. Successful managers learn to use assertiveness rather than either non-assertion or aggression. Generally the more successful the manager, the more assertive they tend to be.

Assertiveness is about speaking your mind openly and objectively, without being over-emotional or using emotional blackmail. It means you can say no (or yes) clearly and firmly, without causing offence, and take responsibility where necessary. An important reason why you may need to develop your assertiveness is because of the extent of your strategic thinking.

As you learn to think strategically, you will start asking important questions about the future of the organisation. This may not make you particularly popular with some fellow managers who are more obsessed with the day to day. Faced with possible criticism for strategic thinking you will need to be able to stand up for your right to think about the future. Thus, in essence, assertion is about *standing up for your rights*.

Assertion means:

● expressing your needs, preferences and feelings without threatening or punishing others
● acting without undue fear or anxiety
● acting without violating the rights of others
● direct, honest communication between individuals interacting equally and taking responsibility for themselves.

Non-assertion means:

● having difficulty standing up for yourself
● voluntarily relinquishing responsibility for yourself
● inviting persecution by assuming the role of victim or martyr.

Aggression means:

● standing up for your rights while violating the rights of others in the process
● promoting yourself at the expense of putting down or humiliating others
● manipulation, which includes subterfuge, trickery, seduction and subtle forms of revenge.

Why you need to be assertive

You need to be assertive because you often face tricky situations at work. These may require you to deal with issues without being disrespectful or making the other person feel humiliated. For example, you might:

● be asked to do something unreasonable by your boss
● feel angry about a lack of co-operation from other people
● need to communicate an unpopular decision
● wish to challenge the view someone senior to you is expressing
● deal with an angry customer without losing valuable business or making promises that are hard to keep
● make a presentation to an important audience with little time to pre-pare.

Many managers either rely on aggression to deal with difficult situations or resort to passivity and a quiet life. Behaving in either of these ways is unlikely to enhance your career in the long run. The third way, being assertive, is both more satisfying and more effective.

Underpinning most assertive behaviour is the simple principle of persistence. You do not just take no for an answer. Instead of merely wishing things were different, you keep on trying to make them so. Rather than giving up when you do not immediately get what you want, you keep on demanding.

Persistence can be expressed in many different ways, including through aggression. A boss who never stops demanding more from you and is excessively forceful about doing so may be simultaneously persistent and aggressive. You can be persistent and assertive by simply stating what you want and how you feel. Self disclosure is therefore an important aspect of being assertive.

Valuable though persistence can be, it may still not get what you want. This does not necessarily mean resorting to aggression. Assertive people can be surprisingly unaggressive, yet still obtain the most wonderful results. One famous public speaker invited to attend an international conference, for example, was coming through passport control and was told he could not enter the country. Patiently he explained that he had been invited as a speaker, but the official refused to believe him. He showed the man the conference papers but these cut no ice.

After trying to achieve what he wanted through persistence, the speaker finally just shrugged. 'I suppose I had better just get on another plane and go home then.'

The official was astounded. 'You mean you are just going to turn around and go back?'

'Of course,' came the reply. 'It is not the end of the world if I do not attend the conference.' Faced with such equanimity and lack of confrontation, the official softened and soon allowed the person through. He even offered apologies for the delay!

Victim behaviour

When you are unassertive you tend to act like a victim. Victims behave as if they have no real choice. For example, they find themselves doing things they never wanted to do, while wondering how it happened. They like to avoid conflict and may do so by trying too hard to please. The chart on page 197 shows the difference between the behaviour of a victim and that of a 'chooser' – someone who is assertive.

Chooser and Victim Behaviour

Chooser

A chooser

- works harder – and has more time
- goes straight to the problem
- makes a *commitment*
- knows when to fight hard, and when to give way
- feels strong enough to be friendly
- listens
- respects other people's strengths
- learns from others
- explains
- feels responsible for more than just his/her work
- sets his/her own pace
- uses time to improve
- is not afraid of making mistakes
- focuses on *possibilities* and *solutions*.

Victim

A victim

- is always too busy
- goes around the problem, and never solves it
- promises too readily
- gives way on important issues, or holds on to things that are not work fighting for
- is rarely friendly, and at times can be a petty tyrant
- waits for his/her turn to talk
- focuses on others' weaknesses
- is resistant to others
- makes excuses
- says, 'That's not my job!'
- has only two speeds: full speed ahead, or dead slow
- uses time to avoid criticism
- is afraid of making mistakes, and of what others will say
- focuses on *problems* and *unsolvable issues*.

Victim remarks and behaviour tend to lead to no reward. The best comment is no comment. The highest congratulations is silence, and the most desirable end result is nil.

The more you talk and act like a *chooser*, the more chooser-orientated you will become. Just like a favourite music cassette, the more you play it, the more you know about it, and the better able you are to hum the tunes and recognise the rhythms and harmonies.

In every situation, you are directly responsible for the tapes you play!

Identify Your Tapes

We have all experienced being *choosers* and *victims* at some time in our lives. Our ultimate aim is to be a chooser as often as possible. Of the following 'tapes' listed below, which ones do you recognise most?

A chooser says:	*A victim says:*
Life is good to me.	*Nothing ever goes my way.*
Yes, I will. No, I won't.	*Yes . . . perhaps . . . I'll see.*
I'll find time to do it.	*How do you expect me to find the time to do this?*
Let's get to the heart of the matter.	
I haven't expressed myself clearly.	*Well, it's difficult to say, exactly . . .*
We have different views on . . .	
I'm OK, but there's still room for change and improvement.	*You just don't understand.*
	I'm not changing my mind.
Tell me . . .	*I'm not as bad as some of the others.*
There must be a better way.	
Let's be more flexible about this.	*I have said again and again . . .*
Let's work on a presentation for management.	*We've always done it this way.*
You learn something new every day.	*The memo said . . .*
Let's make it work this time.	*Management will never agree.*
	What about all my years of experience?
	There's no point in trying again.

In the short term, victims reduce their anxiety by avoiding conflict. Because they do not say no to anyone, they avoid feeling guilty about upsetting them. They also tend to feel sorry for themselves, because naturally they are landed with too much work. To compensate, they often express great pride in suffering so much in producing their work.

In the longer term, however, victims lose their self esteem: they do not value themselves as a person. When you feel that way, you seldom take initiatives or face difficult situations.

Victim managers seldom move on or up. Instead they end up being stuck and unable to add value to the business. Victim behaviour shows up in a lack of decisiveness, an inability to face conflict and constant complaining. If you are to avoid this unpleasant fate you need to practise being assertive, and to recognise when you are not.

Being assertive

When you are assertive you stand up for what you want, while respecting other people's rights. You let them know what you think, feel or want, without attacking them verbally or undermining their own self-esteem. Assertive managers say what they think, and tend to be proactive. They are willing to be out in front, taking a public position. These require you to use your personal power. Unlike power that stems from your formal position, personal power depends on how you use your personality, persuasion skills and networking talents. The proactive manager:

- sets an example
- experiments
- gives feedback
- initiates
- leads
- makes things happen
- puts their own reputation on the line
- questions assumptions
- responds
- shows self-reliance
- shows the way
- takes risks
- takes certain actions without requiring approval
- takes responsibility.

Inexperienced managers often complain of having insufficient authority. For example, they may ask, 'How can I be persuasive when I have so little power?' This is to confuse formal power with the informal kind. In fact when you talk to the most senior managers in any organisation they will usually reveal that they have severely limited powers. No matter how important you become in an organisation, you never really seem to have enough power. Being proactive therefore involves taking enough power to achieve what you want. When you do that you acquire authority merely because others end up willing to let you exercise it.

Your power may stem from:

- coercion – getting what you want through fear, threats and punishments
- expertise – your superior knowledge or skills
- role position – your job or location in the organisation

- rewarding – your ability to reward emotionally or financially
- connections – your access to networks, groups and hence social power.

All of these can help you achieve what you want. Each has to be exercised carefully to avoid putting people down or treating them with a lack of respect.

The most obvious sign of non-assertion, therefore, is not being proactive, not acting on your own initiative or constantly avoiding any kind of risk.

Signs of lack of assertion:

- saying little or nothing in meetings
- not mentioning problems you are having in meeting deadlines
- not realising or accepting that you have certain rights (see page 201)
- frequently comparing yourself unfavourably with other people
- being aggressive rather than assertive
- assuming that to be polite you must be non-assertive.

Non-assertive people make rambling statements, are hesitant, with lots of fill-in words like 'um', 'er', and 'maybe'. They also keep offering apologies or ask permission, and seldom use 'I' statements without some additional qualifier. Assertive people, on the other hand, use language that conveys their commitment to achieving what they want.

Signs of assertion:

- using phrases like 'I think', ' I want', 'I feel', 'I prefer'
- making statements that are brief and to the point
- distinguishing between fact and opinion
- criticising constructively, based on fact, without attacking people
- asking what people are thinking, feeling or needing.

Increasing assertiveness

An important step towards becoming more assertive is recognising when you are being non-assertive. Like any skill, from riding a bicycle to public speaking, you can develop your assertiveness and reduce aggressive tendencies by practice. Here are some tips on being more assertive as a manager:

I have the right to

- ask for what I want
- be treated with respect
- be listened to and taken seriously
- be successful
- change my mind without making excuses
- make mistakes and be responsible for them
- express my own feelings and opinions
- say I don't know, or don't understand
- say yes or no without feeling guilty
- occasionally choose not to assert myself
- manage my own time.

- Make requests without apologising for them. Be direct about what you want, without wrapping it up in long sentences or convoluted ideas. Keep it short and do not try to justify your request other than explaining simply why it is important. Do not take refusal personally and respect the other person's right to say no.

- Refuse unwanted requests by saying no. Many managers feel that they cannot refuse their boss, or deny help when someone demands it. This is often because they believe that the other person will be angry or hurt or will not like them any more, or that they have no right to refuse. If you end up saying yes when you really mean no, you are acting non-assertively.

- Disagree by stating your own views. If you do this aggressively you may lose sight of the issue and allow emotions to obscure the fact that you do not disagree as fundamentally as it appears. This prevents you negotiating a mutually satisfactory outcome. Assertive disagreement means that you state your position openly and firmly. You rely on your beliefs while acknowledging that others are entitled to theirs.

- Give praise without being apologetic about it and without hesitation. Excessive praise does not work either; it must come from the heart. When praise is specific, you give the person a picture of your standards and tell them they have achieved them (see page 203).

- Receive praise without shrugging it off or offering praise in return. Accepting praise without aggression also means doing so without being boastful such as: 'Of course it was a good presentation, I always do them well.' To accept praise assertively, simply thank the giver and keep your response brief. Even if you disagree with their praise, you can qualify your reply while still thanking the person.

- Give bad news without delay or being over apologetic. Assume that you have the right to inform the other person of the situation and they have the right to know the reasons.

Positive Assertion Techniques

1 *Broken record.* Say what you want over and over again, calmly, until the other person finally hears it. You should not rehearse arguments or repeat angry feelings; instead, just stick quietly to your point, saying it in various different ways. Use it, for example, when someone keeps refusing to accept your instructions or persists in asking you to do something you do not want to do.

1 *Fogging.* Use this to deal with manipulative criticism. Instead of being aggressive back, you calmly acknowledge the likelihood that there may be some truth in the criticism. But remain in charge of yourself and the judgement about what you do. It allows you to receive criticism without being anxious or defensive. You respond by agreeing with the person, wrapping up your agreement in constantly changing ways. 'Yes I could certainly have done that better', 'Yes I agree, I'll really have to try harder to get it right next time', 'It's awful, I got it so wrong.'

1 *Counter behaviour.* We tend to mirror other people's behaviour, often quite unconsciously. By becoming more aware of this you can be more assertive and avoid aggression. For example, suppose someone is acting aggressively towards you, pointing a finger, talking in a loud voice, waving their arms. Rather than doing the same you consciously choose to relax, breathe deeply, and talk in a calm manner.

Aggression

Many managers think that to be successful they must be aggressive. Often this is because they have seen apparently successful senior people behaving that way. More often, however, such managers have succeeded *despite* their aggression. People have tolerated it only because they have other valuable talents.

People who act aggressively at work usually obtain some kind of direct or indirect reward from doing so. For example, they see people caving in to their demands or failing to argue. At some level the person concludes that it pays to be aggressive. But does it? Aggressive managers may temporarily get people doing what they want but it seldom lasts. The aggression does not gain their true commitment, and without that you can never get the best from people.

You may tend to act aggressively for a variety of other reasons, for example because you:

● see situations or other people as threatening

● have previously been non-assertive and are reacting against this

● are responding with emotions left over from a previous incident

● need to develop your assertiveness skills.

While aggression can certainly work in some situations, there is usually a high price to pay in poor relationships and your own well being. It often leads to stress, as a result of which you do not think particularly rationally. Hence you risk bad judgement or poor decisions.

Signs of aggression:

● constantly using 'I' statements

● offering opinions as facts

● using threatening questions

● issuing requests as instructions or threats

● giving advice in the form of 'ought' or 'should'

● putting the blame on others

● making assumptions

● using sarcasm or put-downs.

Praise and criticism

An important part of being an assertive manager is being able to offer praise and constructive criticism. You are not alone if you feel slightly uncomfortable with doing either, since the reaction to both can often be quite emotional. You may therefore be tempted to shy away from these two important management responsibilities.

Managers who fail to praise are only too common. Successive surveys in organisations right across the Western world underline that people often feel unappreciated and insufficiently recognised for their efforts. Yet when you explore what makes a really successful top manager they nearly all know how to hand out praise in a way that is genuine and unforced.

Being able to praise someone honestly without doing it grudgingly is good management, and means that you are being assertive. When you offer such praise you are tapping into your own humanity and to avoid giving praise when it is deserved can be as damaging to you as to the other person.

Similarly, people are entitled to know when they are not living up to your standards. You cannot expect them to somehow guess this; you must tell them. Telling someone that what they are doing is not what you wanted, or is making you feel bad in some way, can be as helpful to them as to you. However it also matters how you convey that information.

Faced with someone who is not performing well, you are being non-assertive if you either avoid raising the issue or do so in a tentative, apologetic manner. You are being aggressive if you work yourself up into an angry state and then raise the issue in an abrupt, heavy-handed way.

For criticism to be offered assertively, it needs to be specific, preferably with examples, and not made as a personal attack on the other person. Much the same, incidentally, applies to praise. General, ill-defined praise is usually too diffuse to sound convincing.

Meetings

In meetings you have certain basic rights that you are entitled to assert regularly. For example, you have the right to

- state your opinions and make suggestions
- be listened to and receive a response
- understand what is being said
- disagree
- make your contribution without being interrupted.

You may also be entitled to know how long the meeting will last, know in advance what it is about, receive accurate minutes and attend only those parts directly in your sphere of interest.

Being assertive in meetings is therefore not just about speaking up. It involves ensuring that you obtain all those entitlements that will enable you to make an effective contribution. No one has the right to make you ineffective in a meeting.

Other assertive behaviour in meetings includes helping the meeting along, for example by suggesting a flip chart, asking for a few minutes to study any pages of information that have been handed out, requesting a summary when you feel the meeting is getting bogged down. When you ask for clarification, seek other people's reactions or say you agree with other people, you are also being assertive.

There are also non-verbal ways of being more assertive in meetings that you will find it helpful to consider, for instance giving more eye contact, using above the table hand movements to emphasise your point, using body movements such as sitting forward or sitting back in your chair to signal to others the extent of your involvement.

Further reading

BACK K. and K. *Assertiveness at Work*. 2nd edition. London, McGraw-Hill, 1991

SMITH M. J. *When I Say No I Feel Guilty*. London, Bantam Books, 1985

Index